Night and Day

A Comparative Study of Christianity and Islam

By Andrew Roberts

1st printing 2004, 2nd printing 2005
ISBN: 978-0-9774754-0-7

www.spiritbuilding.com for more tracts and study helps

SPIRITBUILDING PUBLISHING
15591 N. State Rd. 9, Summitville, Indiana, 46070

Spiritual "equipment" for the contest of life.

Author's Note

I thank my wife Julie for her love, companionship, and encouragement.
I thank my brother, Jonathan, for his keen editorial eye in sharpening this work.
I thank Carl McMurray and the Spiritbuilding Publishing team for this opportunity.

I hope this study is received in the spirit with which it is presented: as an honest attempt to open the Bible and the Qur'an, let them speak, and listen closely. This is an introduction, and documentation has been provided to aid and encourage the reader in further examination of Christianity and Islam. I would strongly suggest readers examine the works cited in this text and further explore and educate themselves.

This study is careful, courteous, and candid. I am a Christian, and my conviction is that people dare not "agree to disagree" on Islam and Christianity. If you are looking for a fair comparison with genuine answers to questions of eternal significance, then this study is for you.

Andrew Roberts
December, 2004

Night and Day

A Comparative Study of Christianity and Islam

Contents PAGE

Lesson 1
People of the Book

"Then he took the Book of the Covenant and read in the hearing of the people. And they said, 'All that the LORD has said we will do, and be obedient,'" Exodus 24:7.

Welcome To the Study

There is a God, a Creator of the universe. He fashioned this world and all that is within it. He is not aloof toward His creation, but rather has revealed Himself to those made in His image, humankind. This revelation of Himself and His will for His creation is written and collected as scripture. There is a book.

Succinctly stated, the "people of the book" is that group of adherents or disciples that surrender and submit their will to conform to God's will as expressed in His revelation, the Scriptures. However, "the people of the book" is a loaded phrase in the religious world today. Its meaning depends upon which book one believes to be the inspired, unadulterated word of God. Here the definitive differences of Islam and Christianity begin.

Walking Bibles

Members of the Lord's church have diligently pursued being "people of the book." This is evident by their insistence upon scriptural authority. The motto "give book, chapter, and verse" summarizes the position that the Bible, when "rightly divided" and applied, is the absolute standard and must be appealed to for authority in matters of Christian work, worship, and organization. A consequence of this position is that man-made creeds, confessions, dogmas, or even papal seals are no substitute for the authority of Scripture, Matthew 15:8-9.

This is not to suggest that Christians view the Bible as pertaining merely to Sunday-only religious rites. The Bible is relevant to daily life. Christians have active devotional lives and believe that God, through precept and principle of the Bible, dictates their daily walk in life, Jeremiah 10:23; Psalm 119:105; 2 Peter 1:3. So they pursue the word of God through various avenues: memorization of Scripture, daily Bible reading, regular Bible classes, and listening to gospel preaching, to name a few.

Christians once had the reputation of being "Walking Bibles." It was told in jest that if a copy of a Bible could not be procured for proceedings in court, find a Christian and have the witness place his left hand on him to take the oath. Such a reputation is only earned by diligent Bible study, faithful life application, and the ability to teach and explain the Bible to others. As A. Hugh Clark once counseled a preacher, "Son, you should always have two Bibles with you, one in your pocket and one in your head."[1] Many Christians rightly desire to be, "people of the book."

Who Are The People of the Book?

"O people of the book, Our Apostle has come to you, announcing many things of the Scriptures that you have suppressed, passing over some others. To you has come light and a clear book from God," Surah 5:15.[2]

"The revelation of this Book is from God, the mighty and all-wise," Surah 46:2.

As the Qur'an states in the above passages, it claims to be the inspired word of Allah, who has revealed the Book (his body of scripture) to different people groups at different times in the past, but ultimately gave the correct revelation of his will to his prophet Muhammad. In the Qur'an, Jews and Christians are identified as the former recipients of Allah's word.

"We sent down the Torah which contains guidance and light, in accordance with which the prophets who were obedient (to God) gave instructions to the Jews, as did the rabbis and priests, for they were the custodians and witnesses of God's writ," Surah 5:44.

"Let the people of the Gospel judge by what has been revealed in it by God. And those who do not judge in accordance with what God has revealed are transgressors," Surah 5:47.

Christians and Jews are called *ahl al-kitab* ("the people of the book"). Thus, Muhammad instructs Muslims to treat them fairly, respect the common god, Allah, and heed all scripture (the Old Testament, New Testament, and Qur'an).

"Do not argue with the people of the book unless in a fair way, apart from those who act wrongly, and say to them: "We believe what has been sent down to us, and we believe what has been sent down to you. Our God and your God is one, and to Him we submit," Surah 29:46.

As this Surah continues, it seems that there is an expectation that the people of the book will recognize Muhammad as a true prophet and the authority of his revelations. At least those with honest hearts will.

"That is how We have revealed this Book to you; and those to whom We have sent down the Book will believe in it. Only those who are infidels will deny it," Surah 29:47.

According to the Qur'an, Christians and Jews should see that they are needlessly divided. If these groups would both recognize Muhammad and submit to Islam, then Allah would unite them all as Muslims.

"Those among the people of the book who disbelieve, and the idolaters, would not have been freed (from false beliefs) until the clear proof came to them – An Apostle from God, reading out hallowed pages containing firm decrees. The people of the book were not divided among themselves till after the clear proof had come to them. They were commanded only to serve God with all-exclusive faith in Him, to be upright, and to fulfill their devotional obligations, and to give zakat; for this is the even way. Surely the unbelievers among the people of the book and the idolaters, will abide in the fire of Hell. They are the worst of creatures," Surah 98:1-6.

Yet the harshest punishments are pronounced on those "people of the book" who do not accept Muhammad's prophethood, or who refuse to respect the Qur'an as true scripture. Such dangerous people of the book may try to convert Muslims out of Islam and lead them astray into Christianity or Judaism. This is a clear rejection of Allah's will and Muhammad's message in the Qur'an.

"Say: 'O people of the book, why do you reject the word of God when God is a witness to all that you do?' Then say: 'O people of the book, why do you turn the believers away from the path of God, looking for obliquities in the way when you are witness to it? And God is aware of all that you do.' O believers, if you follow what some people of the book say, it will turn you into unbelievers even after you have come to belief. And how can you disbelieve? To you are being recited the messages of God, and His Prophet is among you. And whosoever holds fast to God shall verily be guided to the path that is straight," Surah 3:98-101.

In fact, even in the early seventh century A.D., most Christians and Jews (apart from some on the Arabian Peninsula coerced by terror and violence) did not recognize Muhammad as a prophet in the biblical tradition nor his "revelations" as worthy of the canon of Scripture. No reason, evidence, or sign has been produced to cause this view to change in the ensuing 1300 years.

Night and Day

Christianity and Islam are exclusive faiths. We grant them the dignity of their claims by recognizing this fact. Honest evaluation of these beliefs is made by admitting their differences and exploring them.

These religions are *Night and Day* different. Both claim to be the light while the other languishes in spiritual darkness, leading souls astray. Their scriptures make this clear:

"I have come as a light into the world, that whoever believes in Me should not abide in darkness. And if anyone hears My words and does not believe, I do not judge him; for I did not come to judge the world but to save the world. He who rejects Me, and does not receive My words, has that which judges him -- the word that I have spoken will judge him in the last day," John 12:46-48.

OR

"God is the friend of those who believe, and leads them out of the darkness into light; but the patrons of infidels are idols and devils who lead them from light into darkness. They are the residents of Hell, and will there for ever abide," Surah 2:257.

"But even if we, or an angel from heaven, preach any other gospel to you than what we have preached to you, let him be accursed. As we have said before, so now I say again, if anyone preaches any other gospel to you than what you have received, let him be accursed," Galatians 1:8-9.

OR

"And We have sent you with the truth to give glad tidings and to warn. You will not be questioned about those who are inmates of Hell. The Jews and Christians will never be pleased with you until you follow their way. Say: 'God's guidance alone is true guidance;' for if you give in to their wishes after having received the (Book of) knowledge from God, then none will you have as friend or helper to save you. Those to whom We have sent down the Book, and who read it as it should be read, believe in it truly; but those who deny it will be losers," Surah 2:119-121.

Helpful Vocabulary

For our comparative study of Islam and Christianity, it is understood that the primary audience is mostly Christian, or at least holds greater familiarity with the Christian faith. All quotations from the Bible will come from the New King James Version unless otherwise stated.[3] All quotations from the Qur'an will come from *AL-QUR'AN: A Contemporary Translation* by Ahmed Ali, unless otherwise stated.[4]

It is encouraged that students obtain their own copy of an English Qur'an for reading, comparing translations, and making their own notes. This study seeks to be as open and fair as possible by allowing the Bible and the Qur'an to speak. Further reading of the Qur'an and Bible will only enhance the process.

There is not a standardized system for numbering the Qur'an's verses. All English translations follow similar guidelines, so if the verse in your English Qur'an does not follow the quotation given in this workbook, simply look to the verses immediately before or after the quotation and you will find it.

A basic vocabulary is needed to make a meaningful comparison between Christianity and Islam. Over the course of this study, definitive differences will be recognized and examined. New words and doctrines will be introduced which pertain to each lesson. As the study begins, here are some helpful definitions for readers to keep in mind.

- Islam – the religion of submission to Allah
- Muslim – one who submits, an adherent of Islam
- Allah – Arabic for the strictly Unitarian God of Islam

- Muhammad – Allah's greatest and final messenger: "The Seal of the Prophets"
- Qur'an – the Holy Book of Islam. Consisting of 114 Surahs, it was revealed by Muhammad
- Surah – Arabic for revelation or recitation. A Surah is synonymous with "chapter" in the Qur'an
- Hadith – Traditions, these are uninspired records of the deeds and teachings of Muhammad. They are relied upon to learn his example, which must be emulated by Muslims, for the Qur'an lacks much narrative about him.
- mosque – the buildings erected for a congregation of Muslims to meet for prayer and instruction from the Qur'an.
- Imam – a prayer leader at the Mosque
- Mullah – teacher and preacher of Islamic doctrine

Our Course of Study

The purpose of *Night and Day: A Comparative Study of Christianity and Islam* is to present a study suitable in length and content for the average person in a small-group or Bible Class setting to 1) receive a clear presentation of each faith from primary sources (the Bible and the Qur'an) for both these works are understandable by their own admission, Surah 12:1-3; Ephesians 3:1-5; 5:17; 2) gain an appreciation of the first principles of both faiths (their history, claims, and precepts); 3) identify definitive differences; and 4) discover the implications of committed discipleship to these mutually exclusive religions.

Christian, Muslim, or Just Curious?

For Christians, this study affirms basic Biblical teaching on the Godhead, Jesus Christ, salvation, the church, and the great commission to take the gospel into the world. Christians will be challenged by considering how "outsiders" view their faith and practice. Christians must address Islam, for it claims to be absolute truth, and is growing in what have historically been "Christian" nations. Christians mindful of "contending for the faith" should know with whom they will contend in the twenty-first century.

For Muslims, this study seeks to be fair. Just as attacks upon the Bible must be examined and answered, so too the Qur'an is neither above question nor investigation. The reason is quite simple. The Qur'an claims that Allah revealed the Bible, and furthermore, Muslims are to receive it as scripture:

"Do not argue with the people of the book unless in a fair way, apart from those who act wrongly, and say to them: "We believe what has been sent down to us, and we believe what has been sent down to you. Our God and your God is one, and to Him we submit," Surah 29:46.

However, Muslims openly question and attack the authenticity and authority of the Bible whenever it opposes Qur'anic teaching. They claim Jews and Christians have tampered with it and re-written great portions to coincide with their unique religious beliefs. Consider: if Allah could not protect his previous holy books from being polluted by interpolations (regardless of who may have done it), as Muslims claim happened to the Bible, surely he can do no better for the Qur'an. It must be examined and tried every bit as rigorously as the Bible for truth. That is fair.

For those seeking genuine answers to questions about God, truth, or salvation, this study invites you to examine the teachings of the Qur'an and the Bible for yourself. This is a simple investigation and discussion. Learn what the sources actually say and make informed choices about your allegiance and the destiny of your soul. Biblical Christianity and Islam both make claims to be absolute truth. Truth has nothing to fear from examination.

Lesson 1 Questions

1. What do you hope to gain from this study of Islam and Christianity?

2. List any questions you have about Islam or Christianity that you hope will be answered during the course of this study.

3. Why might Christians desire to be known as "people of the book"?

4. What kind of commitment to the Bible might earn one the nickname of "Walking Bible" or "a person of the Book"?

5. In your opinion, are many Christians today interested in being "a person of the Book"? Why or why not?

6. Who does Islam label "the people of the book"?

7. Why are these people-groups called "the people of the book"?

8. What did Muhammad say about "the people of the book" that did not accept him as a genuine prophet?

9. What scriptures teach that Christianity is the light and competing religions are darkness?

10. What verses of the Qur'an teach that Islam is the light and competing religions are darkness?

11. Is it possible that the Bible and the Qur'an are both correct on this point?

12. Were there any definitions in the vocabulary section that surprised you? What words (if any) meant something other than what you thought they meant?

13. Define Islam:

14. Define Muslim:

15. What is a Surah?

Endnotes
[1] Bowman, Dee. Common Sense Preaching. Temple Terrace, FL: Florida College Press, 1999. p.111.
[2] Ali, Orooj Ahmed. Al-Qur'an: A Contemporary Translation. Princeton, NJ: Princeton University Press, 1993.
[3] The Holy Bible: The New King James Version. Nashville, TN: Broadman & Holman Publishers, 1996.
[4] Ali, Orooj Ahmed. Al-Qur'an: A Contemporary Translation. Princeton, NJ: Princeton University Press, 1993.

Lesson 2
With God, it's All or Nothing

"(For you shall worship no other god, for the LORD, whose name is Jealous, is a jealous God)," Exodus 34:14.

That Infamous Day

Tuesday, September 11, 2001 – 8:45 a.m. (EDT) American Airlines Flight 11 out of Boston, Massachusetts, crashes into the north tower of the World Trade Center, tearing a gaping hole in the building and setting it afire. Nearly every American remembers where they were on 9/11 when they heard that terrible news. As television broadcasts began live coverage of the "accident," many began to speculate about the cause of what was sure to be one of the greatest disasters in commercial aviation history.

How could this have happened? Had the pilot suffered a heart attack? Had an air traffic-controller fallen asleep at his post? Had there been a malfunction in the plane's navigational system? Communications system? Both? What strange course of events could have resulted in such a horrific plane crash?

These questions became irrelevant as United Airlines Flight 175 from Boston crashed into the south tower of the World Trade Center and exploded at 9:03 a.m. Both buildings were now burning. It was evident to all who witnessed the second plane crash that this was no accident. Over the next hour and a half, two more planes would crash (American Airlines Flight 77 into the Pentagon and United Airlines Flight 93 into a Pennsylvania field), signaling that America was under attack. But who was responsible?

Who Was Responsible?

It was not a Cold-War era enemy. It was not a sovereign nation at all. The days and weeks following these attacks uncovered the culprits as a terrorist group known as Al-Qaeda led by an exiled Saudi-Arabian Muslim terrorist named Osama Bin Laden. The U.S. news media was quick to inform the nation that these men were radical Islamic fundamentalist zealots. U.S. politicians characterized them as a militant, fringe faction of Islam. They were not the product of sound Qur'anic teaching, and their primary goal was to spread terror. We were told their actions were not representative of Islamic faith or practice. But was this flood of information true?

If these men read the Qur'an in the same fashion you read the Bible, would you consider them "radical" or "zealots"? Perhaps you would merely say, "orthodox" or "faithful." This is what their revelation (the Qur'an) says:

"But when these months, prohibited (for fighting), are over, slay the idolaters wheresoever you find them, and take them captive or besiege them, and lie in wait for them at every likely place," Surah 9:5.

"Fight those people of the book who do not believe in God and the Last Day, who do not prohibit what God and His Apostle have forbidden, nor accept divine law, until all of them pay protective tax in submission," Surah 9:29.

It is unsettling, but true: these terrorist attacks were religiously provoked. Their purpose was to spread Islam through the conduit of terror, not spread terror for its own sake. This is not to suggest that every Muslim reads the Qur'an as literally as the Al-Qaeda terrorists, or that those who do act in accordance with its violent precepts. Nor is it suggested that all Muslims share some guilt or responsibility for the actions of a few on September 11. As Mabry points out, "many moderate Muslims, especially in this country, say that Islam is a religion of peace, and they claim to be deeply embarrassed by Islamic acts of terror, which in their view, cannot be justified by the Qur'an."[1] Christians in the United States should not fear their Muslim neighbors nor abuse them in any way, 2 Timothy 1:7; Matthew 5:39, 43-48. However, Christian citizens should seek out and demand a forthright presentation of Qur'anic Islam so they can respond appropriately.

Christians should pray for wisdom on behalf of national leaders that peace may prevail, 1 Timothy 2:1-2. Remember that government serves as God's ministers for good; pray that those in authority won't be deceived by misinformation veiling the violent dangers of Islam, Romans 13:1-7.

Sadly, there remains a vacuum of knowledge (of any kind) about Islam for many Americans, and in the rush to fill this void with information that will calm public tension and protect U.S. Muslims from violence, much misinformation has been spread.

Feeling Misinformed? Go To the Source
An example of this was the Oprah Winfrey broadcast entitled "Islam 101" that aired October 5, 2001 – not even a full month after the attacks, and before U.S. troops were committed in Afghanistan. She interviewed a panel of Muslims (including thirty-one-year-old Queen Rania of Jordan) who were to "educate the audience" about Islam. By listening to this panel you could learn that "Islam views women as full and equal partners to men, so [women's] rights are guaranteed by Islam." You could also learn that wearing a veil is optional for women.[2] The Qur'an denies both statements.[3]

Have you heard these or similar statements of misinformation:
- Islam means "peace."
- Islam and Christianity are sister faiths.
- Muslims believe the Bible as well as the Qur'an.
- Muslims and Christians serve and pray to the same God.
- Muslims believe in Jesus, too.

As we shall see, like those statements about women's rights and wearing veils, the Qur'an and Hadith (authoritative sources of Muslim precept and practice) do not teach or support much of the media's reports on Islam.

The Middle East Moves West

Besides questions about national security (the government's responsibility), people should be asking about faith, truth, and Islamic influence. There is an opportunity for dialogue among Muslim neighbors and adherents in the United States.

In the popular American psyche, Islam has been largely viewed as an antiquated belief system relegated to the third world Middle East. In recent decades, it had occasionally lashed out in hostility (hijackings, kidnappings, wars in the Middle East, etc.), but by and large it was not something in our "backyard." Many are shocked to learn that Islam has more than one billion adherents the world over.[4] As Caesar Farah wrote, "One out of every six human beings today subscribes to the faith of Islam; he lives within a social structure largely the product of Islam, and he is guided in his daily life by norms and precepts forged in the caldron of Islam."[5] It is estimated that two to eight million Muslims live in the United States.[6]

Consider these facts:
- Islam is the world's second largest religion behind Christianity.[7]
- Over sixty-five nations in the world are Islamic.[8]
- An average of one new mosque opens each week in the United States.[9]
- There are presently 165 Islamic schools, 426 Islamic associations and ninety Islamic publications in the United States.[10]
- There are more Muslims than Methodists in the United States.[11]
- There are more Muslims in the United Kingdom than Methodists and Baptists combined. [12]

But more startling than any statistic about Muslim growth or influence is the recollection that on September 11, 2001, nineteen Muslims killed themselves along with thousands of Americans as an act of religious devotion and commitment to their god! This is surely a shocking and incomprehensible blow to our society's view of religion. How could they do that?

Commitment to "Truth"

On some level, Christians should be able to understand the hijackers' actions. That is not to say that their deeds are in any way defensible, for the Bible clearly condemns murder (Genesis 9:6-7; Exodus 20:13; Matthew 26:52), vigilante vengeance (Romans 12:19), and military force as a means of evangelism, John 18:36. Christians should, however, understand what it is to surrender everything to fulfill the will of God, and that is what the Al-Qaeda pilots believed they were doing.

In the Bible, followers of God were called upon to make great sacrifices in His service, up to and including their lives, Hebrews 11:36-40. Stephen and the apostle James knew of the conviction that surrenders everything for the sake of the Lord, Acts

7; 12:1-2. First century Christians understood that some die for their faith in the word of God, Revelation 6:9-11. Never forget that the Holy Spirit called Christians "living sacrifices" (Romans 12:1-2), and Jesus warned that following Him meant taking up the cross, Luke 14:27.

Were the Bible to command Christians to take life for God's glory, rather than lay it down, Christians would be militant also, if they were genuinely committed to the truth, Psalm 119:151; John 17:17; Colossians 1:5-6; 1 Timothy 3:15. Muslims find themselves in this very predicament and are wholly devoted to an evil deception they believe to be truth:

"You tell the unbelievers in case they desist whatever has happened will be forgiven them. If they persist, they should remember the fate of those who have gone before them. So, fight them till all opposition ends, and obedience is wholly God's. If they desist then verily God sees all they do. But if they are obstinate, know that God is your helper and protector: How excellent a helper, and how excellent a protector is He!" Surah 8:38-40.

"So, when you clash with the unbelievers, smite their necks until you overpower them, then hold them in bondage. Then either free them graciously or after taking a ransom, until war shall have come to end. If God had pleased He could have punished them (Himself), but He wills to test some of you through some others. He will not allow the deeds of those who are killed in the cause of God to go to waste," Surah 47:4.

Whose Truth?

In contrast with this exclusive perspective (there is one right way and it may cost you everything to walk it), the prevalent religious mindset of Western civilization (our society) is characterized as pluralism. In a general sense many people believe there is no such thing as objective and absolute truth. To accept such would mean looking at entire religious systems and making decisions about them: True or False; Right or Wrong; Salvation or Damnation. Rather, many today approach religion with the preconception that all belief systems are more or less equal. As Johnston relates, "Most are functioning under a blind assumption of unity. People would like to believe or accept by faith that all religions are basically the same."[13]

Thus, people do not adhere to a belief system on the basis of "right or wrong," but what "works" for them and what "feels good" to them. Such narcissism and pragmatism is the logical consequence after decades of being told:
- A loving God could never judge or condemn.
- Churches and church doctrine are purely human constructs.
- We're all going to heaven, just on different roads.
- Ethics and morality are situational.
- Do what feels good.
- Worship at the church of your choice.

Planting the Seeds of Pluralism

History testifies that the ecumenical movement among protestant denominations in early twentieth century America allowed the freedom to denominational members to pick and choose aspects of "Christian doctrine" from various churches and piece together their own version of Christianity. This allowed adherents to freely move from one denomination to another without consequence.[14] Consider this quote from the *Handbook of Denominations in the United States, 11th Edition:*

> Sociologists have noticed the strength of this ecumenism in American religion and have concluded that we are now in a "post-denominational" period when religious identity has lost its place in individuals' lives. It is relatively easy for an Episcopalian to join a Lutheran church. Even the conversion from Catholic to Protestant or vice versa no longer carries the weight it did fifty years ago. There has been a tendency toward homogenization of religion as churches learn from each other and adopt successful practices. Most Americans have an eclectic faith, one stitched together from many different threads of tradition and contemporary ideas and attitudes.[15]

The question arises, "If such a cafeteria-styled approach can be taken toward one belief system with impunity, why not another?" Is it really such a far step for the twenty-first century "seeker" to piece-meal together an individual belief system using components from several of the world's religions? Rather than choose and stand upon truth, many of the West's religiously pluralist would mix and match and create their own faith. However, self-styled religion will never truly satisfy nor deliver, Colossians 2:8, 20-23. Johnston writes, "In pluralism the assumptions of inclusiveness are comforting notions because they remove the personal responsibility of an individual having to choose. Yet endless openness produces a stagnation; it works to remind listeners that the essential messages of world beliefs – the core teachings of who God is and what it means to be saved – are not inherently the same."[16]

Jesus said, *"And you shall know the truth, and the truth shall make you free,"* John 8:32. Bible believers must come to terms with the facts that this scripture reveals:

- Truth is objective: it exists independent of individual interpretation.
- Truth is knowable.
- Truth is consequential: knowledge and acceptance liberates, while ignorance or rejection condemns.

Gerry Sandusky illustrated this well when he wrote, "Someone told of a discussion with a man who was reading his Bible. Another man asked him what he was doing. The first man said he was searching for the truth. His friend said he didn't know it was lost, and the reader replied, 'It's not lost, but I am without it.'"[17] The pluralist rejects the notion of absolute and objective truth. Rather, he affirms the existence of many truths, and many ways, all of which originate from the same source and head to the same destination. Yet the pluralist's approach leads to erroneous conclusions about both Islam and Christianity.

The religious pluralist would suggest that Islam and Christianity are sister faiths. However, the dramatic events of September 11, 2001, put the pluralist in a predicament. Why would some Muslims kill adherents of a sister faith? Either these faiths are not practically synonymous, or differences in "interpretation" do matter... or both!

Even more perplexing for the religiously pluralist would be these acts of violent suicide. If nothing is absolute, how could anything warrant a total, personal sacrifice? Is any belief worth a life? Make it personal: what conviction would you die for?

Such pluralism is foreign to Biblical Christianity and Orthodox Islam. Adherents can have meaningful dialogues about the differences, because they understand that they are significant and the salvation of souls hangs in the balance.

Absolute Truth

Islam and Christianity are exclusive faiths. Each insists it is THE truth. Their major tenants are antagonistic to one another. By examining their texts (i.e., the Bible and the Qur'an), none can entertain the notion that these religions are complimentary or "sister faiths" in the least.

Jesus said, *"I am the way, the truth, and the life. No one comes to the Father except through Me,"* John 14:6. Colson succinctly speaks to the supremacy of Christianity as divine in origin and unparalleled in purpose.

> Only Christianity offers a way to understand both the physical and the moral order. Only Christianity offers a comprehensive worldview that covers all areas of life and thought, every aspect of creation. Only Christianity offers a way to live in line with the real world [...] We must understand that God's revelation is the source of *all truth*, a comprehensive framework for all of reality. [18]

Yet the Muslim cannot accept Christ's (and thus Christianity's) paramount claim upon truth and life. Muhammad said, **"It is He [Allah] who sent His Apostle with the guidance and the true way to raise it above all faiths, however the idolaters may dislike it," Surah 61:9.** According to the Qur'an, Islam is the ultimate divine revelation. Farah contends that Islam's superiority is found in its application to every aspect of existence. "The secret of Islam's powerful appeal lies in the fact that it is not only a religion regulating the spiritual side of the believer, but also an all-embracing way of life governing the totality of the Muslim's being."[19]

When two religions claim to be God's truth, and they are at odds, they cannot both be correct. Muslims and Christians should admit this out of respect for one another's convictions as well as concern for the truth. God is not glorified by His people compromising faith, downplaying legitimate differences, or pretending to be "sister faiths" to satisfy the religious pluralism of Western Civilization.

The Trouble of Factions

Truth, by definition, is not contradictory, and if adherents followed the truth, then they should be united. Jesus prayed for such unity among His followers and taught that their unity would be a witness to the world of the truth. "*I do not pray for these alone, but also for those who will believe in Me through their word; that they all may be one, as You, Father, are in Me, and I in You; that they also may be one in Us, that the world may believe that You sent Me,*" John 17:20-21. Yet neither Islam nor Christianity can sustain the claim of true unity with credibility in the eyes of the other.

Is Christ Divided?

In the eyes of Muslims, denominationalism is the undoing of the Christian claim to unity. Craig D. Atwood defines denominationalism thus: "Here is the essence of denominationalism: diverse religious traditions and organizations that openly compete for adherents while respecting other religious organizations as valid."[20] Admittedly, if Christians were united, then there would not be great diversity of tradition, there would not be separate organizations, and they would not need to compete among themselves for adherents.

Jesus Christ promised and built one church, Matthew 16:18; Ephesians 1:22-23; 2:11-22; 4:4; 5:23-24. This is in contrast to the 200 "churches" chronicled in the *Handbook of Denominations* and the general acceptance of the denominational arrangement.

In contrast with the idea that "church doctrine" comes from man and is a source of division, sound doctrine (Apostolic teaching) comes from the Holy Spirit. This is what birthed the church. Read Acts 2 and notice the order: The inspired Peter preached the word to sinners (Acts 2:1-36); the sinners responded to the word to be saved (Acts 2:37-41); those converts constituted the church (Acts 2:41, 47); the church continued in the word – the Apostle's doctrine, Acts 2:42-47. Thus they were saved and united by the word of God, 1 Peter 1:22-25; Romans 6:17-18; Ephesians 4:4-6; Jude 3. Restoring the authority of the word of God to its proper place in Christian faith and practice is the only way "Christians" can stand united as a credible witness of the truth, not only to Muslims, but to the world in general.

Islamic Sects

But Muslims fair no better in their witness to unity. There are at least 73 sects among Orthodox Muslims. They fall within four schools (and their subsequent opposing schools): Qadrites, Sifatites, Kharijites and Shi'ites. These Muslims differ in their views over the following four doctrinal issues: 1) predestination and free will; 2) the divine attributes of God; 3) promises and threats, faith and error; and 4) revelation, reason and the imamate or leadership.[21]

Examining Claims

It is beyond the scope and purpose of this study to explore the peculiarities of existing sects within Islam or Christianity. However, there is a commitment to seeking the truth. As both world religions claim their respective scriptures are the final and true revelation from God, we will investigate their claims, lay them open side by side, and allow the texts to speak for themselves.

We will uncover Biblical Christianity as well as Qur'anic Islam, note their definitive differences, and endeavor to take our stand upon the truth.

Lesson 2 Questions

1. Describe ways that our society has changed in the post-September 11 era.

2. List three specific things that you will pray for on behalf of government leaders relating to national dealings with Islamic countries or organizations.

3. What should be the Christian's attitude toward Muslim neighbors and co-workers, Matthew 22:39; Luke 10:25-37?

4. List some specific things Christians can do to have a greater impact on a society with a growing Muslim population, Matthew 5:13-16.

5. What are some possible reasons for the news media and/or politicians saying things about Islam that contradict the Qur'an's precepts?

6. What are some features of Islam and Christianity that make them incompatible with the societal view of religious pluralism?

7. What three things do we learn about truth from Jesus' teaching in John 8:32?

8. Define denominationalism.

9. How has denominationalism catered to and/or encouraged religious pluralism?

10. How is denominationalism contrary to Biblical teaching on "church" and "doctrine"?

11. Why would the existence of sects discredit claims to having the truth?

Endnotes

[1] Mabry, Gene. An Introduction to Islam From a Christian Perspective. Missouri City, TX: www.bibleclassmaterial.com, 2002. p.1.

[2] Gabriel, Mark. Islam and Terrorism. Lake Mary, FL: Charisma House, 2002. p. 42-44. Quotations in this paragraph are taken from Gabriel, p. 42-44.

[3] On male and female equality, read Surahs 4:3; 2:229; 4:11; 33:53; 4:34. On the veil, read Surahs 33:59; 33:33; 33:55.

[4] Farah, Caesar. Islam. 6th ed. New York: Barron's, 2000. p.5.

[5] Farah, p.6.

[6] Rhodes, Ron. Reasoning from the Scriptures with Muslims. Eugene, OR: Harvest House, 2002, p. 8. Six million people is a large disparity in figures. Rhodes discusses reasons for the different numbers reported.

[7] Rhodes, p. 7.

[8] Rhodes, p. 7.

[9] Rhodes, p. 7.

[10] Rhodes, p. 7.

[11] Geisler, Norman and Abdul Saleeb. Answering Islam: The Crescent in the Light of the Cross. Grand Rapids, MI: Baker, 1993 p.9.

[12] Rhodes, p. 7.

[13] Johnston, Graham. Preaching To A Postmodern World. Grand Rapids, MI: Baker, 2001 p.99.

[14] Willis, Mike. Passing The Torch. Bowling Green, KY: Guardian of Truth, 2001 p.52-53. This work has an excellent discussion of the Gospel-Doctrine distinction and its consequences which allows for pluralism to exist within protestant denominations. See lessons 5, 8 and 12 for this discussion.

[15] Mead, Frank S. and Samuel S. Hill. Handbook of Denominations in the United States 11th Edition. Nashville, TN: Abingdon Press, 2001, p. 23.

[16] Johnston, p.99.

[17] Sandusky, Gerry. "The Wide and Narrow Way." Jesus for a New Millennium: Studies in the Gospel of Matthew. Ed. Ferrell Jenkins, et al. Temple Terrace, FL: Florida College Bookstore, 2001. p. 198.

[18] Colson, Charles and Nancy Pearcey. How Now Shall We Live?. Wheaton, Ill: Tyndale, 1999. p. xi.

[19] Farah, p.14.

[20] Mead, p.23.

[21] Farah, p.201.

Lesson 3
Searching "Scriptures"

"The entirety of Your word is truth, And every one of Your righteous judgments endures forever," Psalm 119:160.

The Bible at a Glance
It is indisputable that the Biblical canon was closed some 500 years before Muhammad lived. Consider these facts about the Bible.

- The title "Bible" comes from the Greek BIBLIOS meaning books or The Book.
- The Bible was written by forty men over a 1500 year period. These men were mostly strangers, and came from all walks of life. Occupations of Biblical writers include shepherds, statesmen, priests, fishermen, tax collectors, and farmers.
- These men lived in diverse geographical locations. Portions of the Bible were written on three continents: Asia, Africa, and Europe.
- The Bible consists of 66 books: 39 books comprise the Old Testament, and 27 books make up the New Testament.
- It was written in three languages: Hebrew, Koine Greek, and some portions in Aramaic.

Despite the time span of writing, not to mention the great diversity in writers and languages, the Bible stands today without a single, sustainable contradiction. This is no small feat, as the Bible has throughout the ages received the toughest scrutiny of any document ever known. It is axiomatic that truth cannot and does not contradict itself.

How is it possible to achieve such unity of message with such a diversity of writers, circumstances, and length of time? The Bible claims to be inspired; that is, men moved by God the Holy Spirit spoke and wrote as directed. The writers do not claim to be original, creating the storylines or events themselves. Rather, they claim to be honest and faithful messengers of another's account and story. It is the Holy Spirit who revealed the Old Testament, 2 Peter 1:20-21. The Holy Spirit is also credited with revealing the New Testament, 1 Corinthians 2:7-13. It is claimed that all Scripture is inspired – literally, "God breathed," 2 Timothy 3:16-17.

Christians proudly proclaim the Bible is the inspired word of God. It is the truth! The God of the Bible speaks the word of truth, John 17:17. The God of the Bible is not the author of contradiction nor confusion, 1 Corinthians 14:33.

The Qur'an at a Glance

For Muslims, the Qur'an is the "Mother of Books," Surah 43:3-4. Note these facts about the Qur'an.

1. The title "Qur'an" is Arabic and means recite or recitation. The Qur'an was "recited" over a twenty-year period by one author, Muhammad. It is taught that Allah sent it in small portions so it would be easy for others to memorize it, Surah 17:105-106; 87:6.
2. Islam teaches that Muhammad began receiving revelations from Allah at the age of forty (approximately 610 A.D.) and continued receiving until his death (632 A.D.).
3. The Qur'an did not exist in a single written volume during Muhammad's lifetime. It is held that Muhammad could neither read nor write. As he spoke, faithful Muslims would memorize his words or write them down on available materials such as animal bones, leaves, skins, mats, and bark. Uthman, the third Muslim Caliph (644-656 A.D.), selected one written manuscript of the Qur'an and ordered all competing manuscripts, as well as original materials to be burned. Thus, there is no historical, textual criticism in Islam. All ancient variant documents were destroyed.
4. The Qur'an is composed of 114 Surahs. Surah is Arabic for "revelation." The Qur'an is not a series of books like the Bible, but a series of "revelations" composing a single book. It is approximately one-third the length of the Bible.
5. The Surahs vary in length. They are placed in order from longest to shortest, an arrangement which fairly well sets them in reverse chronological order. In actuality, the shorter Surahs, placed toward the conclusion of the Qur'an, were written before those placed at the beginning.
6. The Qur'an was "recited" in two locations: Mecca and Medina, cities on the Arabian Peninsula. Muslim scholars believe 86 of the Qur'an's Surahs were produced in Mecca and 28 were produced in Medina.
7. The Qur'an was recited and written in Arabic. This is significant in the present day. It is still contended by Muslims that to truly read and understand the Qur'an it must be in Arabic.[1] As we shall see, this contention suggests that Arabic is the exclusive language of Allah and Paradise.

The Qur'an claims to be inspired. But the Muslim's concept of inspiration differs from Christian teaching. In Islam, there is no Godhead. Godhead or "trinity" is condemned outright – There is no God the Father, God the Son, God the Holy Spirit, Surah 4:171; 5:73.

"Disbelievers are they surely who say: "God is the third of the trinity;" but there is no god other than God the one. And if they do not desist from saying what they say, then indeed those among them who persist in disbelief will suffer painful punishment," Surah 5:73.

Interestingly, the term 'Holy Spirit' is mentioned three times in the Koran, 2:87, 253; 16:102. In the first two instances, this is the being who strengthens Jesus for His ministry; in the third, it is the one who brings the message of the Koran to Muhammad. Hence, the general consensus among Muslim scholars is that the Holy Spirit is merely another title for the angel Gabriel, because both the Koran and the Islamic tradition claim Gabriel as the agent of God's revelation to Muhammad.[2]

Islamic inspiration follows this line:

> 1. Allah gives the message to an angel.
> 2. Then an angel gives the message to a prophet.
> 3. Then a prophet writes or preaches the message to people.

"Say: 'Whosoever is the enemy of Gabriel who revealed the word of God to you by the dispensation of God, reaffirming what had been revealed before, and is a guidance and good news for those who believe, - Whosoever is the enemy of God and His angels and apostles, and of Gabriel and Michael, then God is the enemy of such unbelievers,'" Surah 2:97-98.

Islam teaches that Gabriel is the angel-messenger who carried portions of Allah's Qur'an to Muhammad. The prophet would then recite them in Arabic, and other Muslims would write them down in that language.

Precious Book

Muslims greatly esteem their holy book, the Qur'an. They study the book, memorize its verses, and receive instruction from it at mosques. They also revere the volume itself.

In a Muslim's house, the Qur'an is to rest on the highest shelf. They kiss the volume and touch it to their foreheads. It is never to touch the ground. In fact, a special stand is constructed to hold it while it is opened and being read. The Qur'an is always to be revered, for it is believed to be Allah's perfect and final revelation from his greatest prophet, Muhammad.

"It is He who sent His Messenger with guidance and the true faith in order to make it superior to other systems of belief, even though the idolaters may not like it," Surah 9:33.

While Christians do not prize their personal copies of the Bible the way Muslims would a Qur'an, their convictions are no less grounded that the Bible is indeed God's complete and final revelation for mankind. The Bible states that THE FAITH has been delivered once and for all time, Jude 3. Furthermore, THE GOSPEL cannot be changed, Galatians 1:6-8; Romans 1:16; Mark 16:15-16.

Who Wrote What?

Obviously, the Qur'an claims to be sent by Allah.

"The revelation of this Book is from God, the mighty and all-wise," Surah 46:2.

The Qur'an also claims that Allah authored the Torah (Old Testament) and the Gospel (New Testament), Surah 3:3. In other words, Allah gave mankind the Bible as well as the Qur'an.

However, Islam does not view this as a progressive revelation or scheme of salvation. Muslims do not teach that God made one religion to the Jews, which was set aside by the religion of Christ, which in turn was set aside by Islam. Rather, they teach that Islam is the one true religion and always has been. It was Islam that was given to the Jews. Later, Islam was taught by Jesus to Christians. (Often Christians are spoken of in the Qur'an as if they were a race like Jews or Arabs, and not a spiritual family made of all races). Islam was then sent a third time to Muhammad, who proclaimed it to the Arabs in the early seventh century A.D., Surah 5:44-48.

"He has verily revealed to you this Book, in truth and confirmation of the Books revealed before, as indeed He revealed the Torah and the Gospel," Surah 3:3.

"Say: 'We believe in God and what has been sent down to us, and what had been revealed to Abraham and Ishmael and Isaac and Jacob and their progeny, and that which was given to Moses and Christ, and to all other prophets by the Lord. We make no distinction among them, and we submit to Him,'" Surah 2:136.

Initially, the Qur'an does not attempt to contradict or supersede the previous scripture. As we see in Surah 2:136, Muslims are told to believe the word sent to Moses and Christ. But it eventually asserts its superiority, Surah 9:33. The Qur'an is called "Mother of Books," Surah 43:3-4. This assertion indicates that Muhammad's message is superior to other Scripture.

"But those who believe and do the right, and believe what has been revealed to Muhammad, which is the truth from their Lord, will have their faults condoned by Him and their state improved," Surah 47:2.

Can God's Word Be Changed?

The Muslim teaching that the Jews were taught Islam, Jesus taught Islam, and Muhammad restored Islam is unsubstantiated. Simply reading the documents destroys the notion. The New Testament does not repeat the Old Testament. The Qur'an does not repeat the New Testament. Actually, the Qur'an retells and revises both the Old and New Testaments, with a slant toward the superiority of Islam and the prophet Muhammad.

If the Muslim claim that all Biblical scripture is from Allah were true, why would the Qur'an be necessary? Would not the Bible be sufficient to teach the world Islam? Why is there a latter revelation? After all, Allah's words cannot be changed, altered, or distorted, according to the Qur'an.

"There is no changing the words of God," Surah 10:64.

"Such was the law of God among those before you; and you will not find any change in the law of God," Surah 33:62.

"There is no changing the word of God: The news of (past) apostles has come to you already," Surah 6:34.

"Perfected are the laws of your Lord in truth and justice, and there is no changing His laws. He is all-hearing and all-knowing," Surah 6:115.

There is a fundamental contradiction in Islam. Just as clearly as the Qur'an states that Allah's word cannot be changed or corrupted, the Qur'an states that Allah's word has been both changed and corrupted by Jews and Christians, Surah 2:53-59! Muslims believe and teach the Bible to be an untrustworthy book, full of interpolations and lies concocted by Jews and Christians. It is formally called the doctrine of *"tahrif,"* the corruption of Jewish and Christian Scriptures.

"We have sent no messenger or apostle before you with whose recitations Satan did not tamper. Yet God abrogates what Satan interpolates; then He confirms His revelations, for God is all-knowing and all-wise. This is in order to make the interpolations of Satan a test for those whose hearts are diseased and hardened: Surely the sinners have gone far in dissent," Surah 22:52-53.

Evidently, Allah did not safeguard his revelation in centuries past and allowed Satan, through the Jews and Christians, to disregard and pollute his scripture. Jews and Christians are condemned for the following:
1. They concealed the word of Allah, Surah 2:42, 146; 3:71, 187.
2. They verbally distorted the word of Allah, Surah 3:78; 4:46.
3. They do not believe all the word of Allah, Surah 2:85.
4. They are ignorant of the word of Allah, Surah 2:78.

Can Allah protect his word from corruption? If the Christians and Jews had polluted the Scripture so terribly in the nearly 600 years between Jesus and Muhammad's birth, what has prevented the Qur'an from being polluted in the 1300 years since Muhammad's death?

Beyond changes made in Allah's word which polluted it, changes were made in Allah's word to improve it! One Hadith (orthodox, authoritative, Islamic tradition) recounts that 'Abdollah b. Abi Sarh, one of Muhammad's scribes, often made suggestions to improve the revelations that Muhammad was dictating to him.

On a number of occasions he had, with the Prophet's consent, changed the closing words of verses. For example, when the Prophet had said "And God is mighty and wise" ('aziz, hakim), 'Abdollah b. Abi Sarh suggested writing down "knowing and wise" ('alim, hakim), and the Prophet answered that there was no objection. Having observed a succession of changes of this type, 'Abdollah renounced Islam on the ground that the revelations, if from God, could not be changed at the prompting of a scribe such as himself. After his apostasy, he went to Mecca and joined the Qorayshites.[3]

Can God's word be changed? Can Allah not transmit and keep his message as he intends? 'Abdollah was right. If the Qur'an were truly of God, it could not be added to, nor subtracted from. Such is the standard of the God of the Bible, Deuteronomy 4:2; Revelation 22:18-19.

The Uncreated

The revisable nature of Muhammad's revelation undercuts another fundamental Muslim doctrine concerning the Qur'an: that it is eternal, uncreated, and inscribed on tablets in Paradise. This is the doctrine of *"ijaz al-Qur'an."* "All Muslims with the exception of the Mu'tazilah accepted the dogma of ijaz al-Qur'an (uncreatedness of the Qur'an). No combination of man or supernatural forces can reproduce a fragment thereof, as it is a work existing from all eternity and unequaled."[4] The teaching finds support in the Qur'an.

"This is indeed the glorious Qur'an (Preserved) on the guarded tablet," Surah 85:21-22.

Muslims contend that the Qur'an is the divine, eternal word of Allah. Like Allah, it was never created. So when Muhammad recited, he recited the eternal words of Allah, verbatim, just as they are inscribed on tablets in Paradise… in Arabic! Muslims conclude that Arabic is the language of Allah and Paradise. Furthermore, they teach that one can gain full understanding of the Qur'an strictly by reading it in Arabic. While this position is insulting to great Muslim minds of other native languages, it raises another concern, as Richardson points out:

> If the Koran makes full sense only in Arabic, it is not a revelation for all mankind – unless Allah (Arabic for "God") requires all mankind to learn Arabic. In fact, teachers in thousands of Muslim madrasas require millions of non-Arab students to memorize the entire Koran in Arabic – a language they do not know or understand! Could this be a cover-up? Keen minds that would be bored or appalled by a pseudo-revelation if they could understand it are left in the dark, knowing only what a mullah – the equivalent of a pastor in Islam – chooses to explain in the local language.[5]

The Qur'an testifies of itself that it is perfect, infallible, and unchangeable.

"Those who reject the Reminder when it has come to them (should know) that it is a Book inviolate. Falsehood cannot enter it from any side: It's a revelation from the all-wise and praiseworthy (God)," Surah 41:41-42.

According to the Muslim doctrine of *"ijaz al-Qur'an,"* there can be no pollution, no falsehood, and no contradiction in the Qur'an.

Contradictions Exist

"Here is the solution to the mystery: The Qur'an is filled with contradictions."[6] Let us note a few glaring internal contradictions:

1. There is a textual discrepancy concerning Muhammad's calling as Allah's prophet:
   • Allah personally appeared as a man calling Muhammad, Surah 53:2-18; 81:19-24.
   • Holy Spirit (Gabriel?) issued the call, Surah 26:192-194.
   • Angels announced the call, Surah 15:8.
   • Solely Gabriel brought the call, Surah 2:97.

Concerning Muhammad's calling, Robert Morey observes, "The Qur'an gives us four conflicting accounts of this original call to be a prophet. Either one of these four accounts is true and the others are false or they are all false. They cannot all be true."[7]

2. Contradiction on Creation:
   • Allah created the world in six days, Surah 7:54; 10:3; 11:7.
   • Allah created the world in two days, Surah 41:9, 12.

3. From what substance did Allah create humans?
   • Allah created humans from nothing, Surah 19:67.
   • Allah created humans from the earth, dust, or clay, Surah 11:61; 3:59; 15:26; 6:2; 7:12.
   • Allah created humans from water, Surah 21:30; 25:54.
   • Allah created humans from a blood clot, Surah 96:1-2.
   • Allah created humans from thick fluid, Surah 16:4; 75:37.

4. The punishment for adultery:
   • Both the adulterer and the adulteress shall receive 100 lashes for the offense, Surah 24:2.
   • Only the adulteress shall be punished by life imprisonment, Surah 4:15.

5. Will Christians be saved in Paradise or damned to Hell?
   • Christians shall enter Paradise, Surah 2:62; 5:69.
   • Christians shall go to Hell, Surah 5:72; 3:85; 98:6.

This list is hardly exhaustive. There are numerous internal contradictions in the Qur'an. Also, if one seriously entertains the notion that the Bible is from Allah as well (as the Qur'an claims), one must be prepared to face the myriad of contradictions that exist between these two books. They are truly irreconcilable.

Abrogation

What about these internal contradictions? How can they not trouble Muslims? Surely they do. Yet Islam answers such concerns with the doctrine of *"naskh,"* or abrogation. "Naskh is based on the fact that the Qur'an was revealed to Muhammad at different times over a period of about twenty-two years. Some parts of the Qur'an came later and some parts came earlier. To solve a contradiction, they decided that new revelations would override (nasikh) previous revelations."[8] In fact, the Qur'an builds in this very defense against contradiction and allows Allah to say things totally contrary to previous revelations.

"When we cancel a message (sent to an earlier prophet) or to throw it into oblivion, We replace it with one better or one similar. Do you not know that God has power over all things?" Surah 2:106.

This shifty and convenient doctrine evidently sounded suspect even in Muhammad's day. In one Surah, Muhammad answered his contemporary critics:

"When we replace a message with another – and God knows best what He reveals – they say: 'You have made it up;' yet most of them do not know," Surah 16:101.

Allah and his prophet, Muhammad, were completely free from the restraint of consistency in teaching or practice.

Some Muslims try to defend the doctrine of abrogation by saying the same was done in the Bible between the Old Testament and the New Testament:

> Many Muslims say that the Bible is no longer applicable. The simplest form of this theory may be put this way:
> As the Injil (Gospel) abrogated the Tawrat (Torah) of Moses, so the Qur'an abrogated the Injil. Abrogation means declaring it null, void, or unnecessary. Therefore, even if genuine copies of the former books exist, there is no need for Muslims to read them.[9]

The Old Testament writings did indeed prophesy that God would establish a new covenant, Jeremiah 31:31-34. This new covenant would be open to Jew and Gentile alike (thus a universal covenant), and the New Testament, the covenant of Christ, is the fulfillment of that prophesy, Hebrews 8:7-13; 2 Corinthians 3:2-18. But where did God ever declare the Old Testament to be "void" or "unnecessary," such as abrogation teaches?

The New Testament declares of the Old Testament:
- It was written for Christians to learn and have hope, Romans 15:4.
- It was written as an example and admonition for Christians,
    1 Corinthians 10:6, 11.
- It makes people wise for salvation in Christ, 2 Timothy 3:14-15.
- It declares and testifies Jesus Christ, John 5:39.
- It is the tutor, leading to Jesus Christ, Galatians 3:24-25.

Jesus, whose sacrifice on the cross ratified the New Covenant, did not claim to abolish or abrogate the Old Testament; rather, He came to fulfill it.

"Do not think that I came to destroy the Law or the Prophets. I did not come to destroy but to fulfill. For assuredly, I say to you, till heaven and earth pass away, one jot or one tittle will by no means pass from the law till all is fulfilled," Matthew 5:17-18.

Jesus did *"fulfill all,"* and finished His work as Messiah (John 19:30), thus taking the Old Law out of the way by the cross, Colossians 2:11-17. Jesus also said, *"the Scripture cannot be broken,"* John 10:35. The truth that God fulfilled His Old Testament prophecies and instated a New Covenant whereby all nations can be saved is not synonymous with the Muslim doctrine of abrogation. Rather, it demonstrates that true Scripture is never broken or recanted. It is fulfilled, Isaiah 55:10-11!

If Christians are to accept that the Qur'an came from God and constitutes a newer, superior truth, where was it prophesied in the New Testament? The Old Testament foretold the New Testament. What scripture tells Christians to look for and hasten the day of Islam? What prophecies of God, foretold in Christianity, find their fulfillment in Islam?

While abrogation may be a hallmark of Muslim scripture, it finds no precursor or justification in the Bible. Rather, all may read in the New Testament:

"Heaven and earth will pass away, but My words will by no means pass away," Matthew 24:35.

"If He called them gods, to whom the word of God came (and the Scripture cannot be broken)," John 10:35.

"I marvel that you are turning away so soon from Him who called you in the grace of Christ, to a different gospel, which is not another; but there are some who trouble you and want to pervert the gospel of Christ. But even if we, or an angel from heaven, preach any other gospel to you than what we have preached to you, let him be accursed. As we have said before, so now I say again, if anyone preaches any other gospel to you than what you have received, let him be accursed," Galatians 1:6-9.

Particular attention should be paid to the passage of scripture quoted above from Galatians. Should Gabriel the angel (or any other man or angel), be responsible for the creation of another religion or system of salvation, both he and his message are declared by the Holy Spirit in the Bible to be accursed (literally, destined for destruction).

Lesson 3 Questions

1. Is it reasonable to believe that the Bible came from God? Why or why not?

2. What languages were the Biblical documents originally written in?

3. What does "Qur'an" mean?

4. What language was the Qur'an originally written in?

5. What is the "process of inspiration," according to Muslims? How is this similar or different to Christian belief about the "process of inspiration?"

6. What is the name of the angel who brought Islam to Muhammad?

7. Consider how Muslims treat copies of the Qur'an. Consider how you treat your Bible. What messages do you think your treatment of the Bible would send to a Muslim neighbor?

8. Where did the Bible come from, according to the Qur'an?

9. Why did Allah send the Qur'an to Muhammad?

10. Discuss particular criticisms that the Qur'an is open to by being strictly Arabic. Would "Christians" be open to similar criticisms for insisting that worship be conducted in Latin or that only the KJV Bible is the "true" word of God?

11. Can Allah's word be changed? How has it been changed?

12. Why did Muslim scribe 'Abdollah b. Abi Sarh "apostatize" and leave Islam?

13. What facts about the Qur'an destroy the notion that it is "uncreated" and infallible?

14. How do Muslims justify the many contradictions throughout the Qur'an?

15. Was abrogation, as seen in the Qur'an, practiced in the Bible?

16. What value is the Old Testament to New Testament Christians?

17. What is said for angels or others who bring alternative gospels into the world, Galatians 1:6-9?

Endnotes

[1] Because there has not been an officially sanctioned translation of the Qur'an from Arabic to another language, Muslim scholars have made their translations independently. This means there is not a standard numbering of verses within the Surahs. If you are studying along with your own copy of the Qur'an, the verses may not exactly match up with the quotations given in this study. But if you look at a verse or two either before or after the verse given, you will find the quotation given in the workbook in your copy of the Qur'an.

[2] Elass, Mateen. Understanding the Koran. Grand Rapids, MI: Zondervan, 2004. p. 62 .

[3] Geisler, Norman and Abdul Saleeb. Answering Islam: The Crescent in Light of the Cross. Grand Rapids, MI: Baker, 1993. p. 157. They quote Ali Dashti. Twenty Three Years. London: George Allen & Unwin, 1985. p. 98.

[4] Farah, Caesar E. Islam 6th ed. New York: Barron's, 2000. p. 101.

[5] Richardson, Don. Secrets of the Koran. Ventura, CA: Regal Books, 2003. p. 90.

[6] Gabriel, Mark A. Islam and Terrorism. Lake Mary, FL: Charisma House, 2002. p. 29.

[7] Morey, Robert. The Islamic Invasion. Las Vegas, NV: Christian Scholar Press, 1992. p. 76.

[8] Gabriel, p. 30.

[9] Saal, William J. Reaching Muslims for Christ. Chicago: Moody Press, 1991. p. 85.

Lesson 4
Establishing Scriptural Authority
in Christianity and Islam

"Hold fast the pattern of sound words which you have heard from me, in faith and love which are in Christ Jesus," 2 Timothy 1:13.

Pattern in the Old Testament

The God of the Bible is the God of peace, not confusion (1 Corinthians 14:33); design, not disorder (Ezekiel 43:10-12); and truth, not contradiction, John 17:17; Psalm 119:151. He is the God of purpose and pattern.

God has always revealed His will to men with patterns. Men were judged righteous by their faithful obedience to the pattern God gave. There are numerous examples of this in the Old Testament; let's look at three:

1. Noah and the Ark, Genesis 6:13-21

God was very specific about the ark. He wanted it made of gopherwood and built to particular specifications. Note how Noah responded:

"Thus Noah did; according to all that God commanded him, so he did," Genesis 6:22. *"And Noah did according to all that the Lord commanded him,"* Genesis 7:5.

God was pleased with Noah, and he and his household were saved by his faithful obedience to the pattern of God, Hebrews 11:7.

2. Moses and the Tabernacle, Exodus 25-27

God was very specific about His tabernacle. He wanted it constructed to particular dimensions with appropriate materials. He even dictated who could come near it and serve. Note these admonitions given to Moses:

"And let them make Me a sanctuary, that I may dwell among them. According to all that I show you, that is, the pattern of the tabernacle and the pattern of all its furnishings, just so you shall make it," Exodus 25:8-9.

"And see to it that you make them according to the pattern which was shown you on the mountain," Exodus 25:40.

Moses is forever commended for acting according to God's revelation. Later in Hebrews 8, Bible students learn how significant it was that Moses followed God's pattern: all the tabernacle elements served as types and shadows of the Christ and God's eternal purpose.

3. The Building of the Temple, 1 Chronicles 22-23; 1 Kings 5-6

God was just as concerned about the building of His temple in Jerusalem for the nation of Israel. He dictated who would lead the building project, Solomon and not David. Furthermore, Solomon was not given free reign to design the temple any way he wanted:

"Then the word of the LORD came to Solomon, saying: 'Concerning this temple which you are building, if you walk in My statutes, execute My judgments, keep all My commandments, and walk in them, then I will perform My word with you, which I spoke to your father David,'" 1 Kings 6:11-12.

In fact, Solomon was given the pattern for building from David, who received it from the Holy Spirit, 1 Chronicles 28:9-12, 19. Notice especially verses 11 and 12:

"Then David gave his son Solomon the plans for the vestibule, its houses, its treasuries, its upper chambers, its inner chambers, and the place of the mercy seat; and the plans for all that he had by the Spirit, of the courts of the house of the Lord, of all the chambers all around, of the treasuries of the house of God, and of the treasuries for the dedicated things," 1 Chronicles 28:11-12.

Because Solomon and David were obedient in these things, all of Israel was blessed by the glory of the Lord descending upon the temple, 1 Kings 8:10-11.

The Law of Moses – God's revelation and covenant to the Israelites – was viewed as the sufficient pattern for their worship, organization, and prosperity under the leadership of God. They were never to add to or subtract from God's word, Deuteronomy 4:2; 12:32. God's Scripture is not amendable.

Many things in life change, but not the principles of God or God Himself, Malachi 3:6; Hebrews 13:8. And like Israel of old, Christians have been given a pattern to follow by God. This pattern is the New Testament.

Pattern in the New Testament

Christians are not left to wonder concerning God's will for His people or His church. By following the teachings and examples of the apostles and other inspired writers, Christians can discern what is acceptable and pleasing before God. It is important to realize that not every work that a man does in the name of God, or as worship to God, is actually pleasing to God, Matthew 7:21-23. That was the lesson Cain learned, Genesis 4:1-7. But by respecting what God has authorized in the work, worship, and organization of His people, His church, God shall be pleased, Colossians 3:17; Hebrews 11:6. Christians accomplish this by following the apostles' doctrine, example, and traditions as recorded in the New Testament – the pattern, Acts 2:42; 1 Corinthians 4:17; 11:1; Philippians 3:17; 4:9; 2 Thessalonians 3:6; 2 Peter 3:1-2.

God, through the New Testament scriptures, authorizes Christian faith and practice in the following ways :[1]

1. Precept or Command. The Bible gives direct statements of God where truths are expressly declared and behaviors are commanded or prohibited, Acts 17:30; Colossians 3:9. Christians are to obey them.

2. Approved Apostolic Example. The Bible recounts the practices of the inspired apostles and of the church in the New Testament that met with God's approval, and Christians are to follow those examples. For instance, Christians should meet on the first day of the week to observe the Lord's Supper, Acts 20:7; 1 Corinthians 11:20-26. A plurality of elders should lead a local church, Acts 14:23; Philippians 1:1; 1 Peter 5:1-2. These practices we learn from the example of the first century church.

3. Necessary Inference. A necessary inference "is something that is neither expressly stated nor specifically exemplified yet is necessarily implied or inferred by the clear import and meaning of the language used."[2] For instance, it is necessarily inferred that Lot went down to Egypt with Abram because it is recorded that he traveled out of Egypt with Abram, Genesis 13:1; 12:10. It is necessarily inferred that Jesus went down into the water to be baptized because it is recorded that He rose up out of the water after He was baptized, Matthew 3:16. With the Lord's Supper, it is necessarily inferred that Christians should meet to observe it every first day of the week. When we compare the example of Acts 20:7 for Christians with the command of Moses to the Israelites to keep the Sabbath (Deuteronomy 5:12), we see that when God specifies a day of the week for something, then every time that day rolls around, it is to be observed.

By adhering to this three-fold method of respecting and establishing scriptural authority, much confusion and disagreement within "Christendom" might be resolved. It is important to recognize the consistency in the manner of revelation and interpretation of the followers of God as recorded in both the Old and New Testaments. The God who revealed the Old Testament and New Testament revealed an unalterable pattern for His people to follow, Deuteronomy 4:2; 2 Timothy 1:13; Revelation 22:18-19. Surely if the Qur'an is the most recent and pure revelation from God (as it claims to be) then the same emphasis on pattern and manner of obedience would be consistent within it.

In other words, the Qur'an should constitute an unalterable pattern in worship and practice, and Muslims should study it diligently and adhere to its commands, examples, and necessary conclusions. This is consistent with the way Scripture was handled by Israelites and Christians as recorded in the Bible.

Some Surahs suggest that Muhammad's recitations provide such a standard for Muslims.
"No believing men and women have any choice in a matter after God and

His Apostle have decided it. Whoever disobeys God and His Apostle has clearly lost the way and gone astray," Surah 33:36.

Yet upon investigation, Islam's revelations are lacking in every respect when compared to the Biblical basis for establishing scriptural authority.

The Effect of Abrogation upon the Authority of Precepts

Recall that the Islamic doctrine of abrogation essentially allows Allah to say things entirely contradictory to previous "revelations." He can do this both with written scripture (he can contradict the Bible that he supposedly revealed – Surah 3:3) or earlier teachings (verbal sayings) of Muhammad.

"When we cancel a message (sent to an earlier prophet) or to throw it into oblivion, We replace it with one better or one similar. Do you not know that God has power over all things?" Surah 2:106.

"When we replace a message with another – and God knows best what He reveals – they say: 'You have made it up;' yet most of them do not know," Surah 16:101.

So which commands does Allah expect people to follow? When conflicting precepts occur, which one is the faithful Muslim to keep? Muhammad did not specifically identify every command Allah repealed. Mark Roberts notes that "Muhammad used the law of abrogation in Sura 2:142-144 to change the direction of prayer from Jerusalem to Mecca. Many of the so-called 'sword' verses (Sura 9:5; 47:4; 9:29) are abrogations of the earlier command, 'there is no compulsion in religion' (Sura 2:256). Examples of this kind can be multiplied. Allah's word to Muhammad is not very sure and certain!" [3]

Evidently, Muslim scholars must operate off a rule of thumb: when a contradiction occurs, those Surahs revealed later in Muhammad's life should supersede the ones revealed earlier in his life. Such is a tall order, as all ancient manuscripts, variant manuscripts, and original materials were burned in lieu of the canon chosen by Caliph Uthman. Much of the historical evidence that would substantiate the dates and sequence of particular Surahs has been lost.[4]

Not only does this state of things cause Muslims difficulty in knowing which commands to obey, but it is partly responsible for misinformation spread about Islam. It has been said of the Bible that one can make it support any position by wresting scriptures from their context. Because of abrogation, and the lack of textual criticism upon ancient manuscripts, this is doubly true for the Qur'an! It is very difficult to know whether a Surah is being wrested from its context to prove a position. Some Muslims will say that peace-oriented Surahs prevail over militant Surahs (which are mostly limited to the context of wars Muhammad personally led). Other Muslims contend that jihad Surahs stand without any abrogation. Don Richardson expands upon the implications of the difficulty:

Frequent media reports tell of Muslims forcing non-Muslims to convert to Islam at the muzzle of an AK-47. Muslim apologists are quick to say such reports must be false because Mohammed himself commanded, "There shall be no compulsion in religion," Koran 2:257. Surely that is a peace verse in the Koran.

Not really. Muslims who quote 2:257 also know that it has been abrogated (i.e., annulled, cancelled, replaced) by the very one who initially gave it – the Muslims' God – in at least 109 other verses. Remember, the Muslim doctrine allows God (Mohammed actually) to affirm something positive and then abrogate it with something negative. This is what makes it difficult – impossible really – for us to trust any good verse any Muslim apologist ever quotes from the Koran. [5]

When the Qur'an brings forth contradictory commands or prohibitions, which shall the Muslim choose to keep? Clearly abrogation has a profound impact upon the binding authority of precepts in Islamic scripture.

The Effect of Divine Favoritism upon the Authority of Apostolic Example

The New Testament holds up the conduct and teaching of the apostles as examples intended for Christians to follow, 1 Corinthians 11:1; Philippians 4:9; 1 Thessalonians 1:5-6; 2 Thessalonians 3:7. It is important to note, also, that these examples are easier for the Christian to accept and follow because the apostles were not a rule unto themselves. The apostles Jesus chose as special ambassadors of the gospel (2 Corinthians 5:20) were not above the message they preached. They could yet sin and stand condemned, as Peter did, Galatians 2:11-21. They could be disqualified to receive the imperishable prize for which they strove (1 Corinthians 9:25-27), and they would be held accountable (as will all) to the word of God, 2 Corinthians 5:10-11; John 12:48.

Muhammad is the apostle of the Qur'an that Muslims are told to emulate. Other figures, such as Abraham and Jesus, are mentioned in the Qur'an as worthy examples to follow, Surah 60:4; 43:59, 63. However, Muhammad is ultimately the "Seal of the Prophets" and the model Muslim.

"You have indeed a noble paradigm in the Apostle of God for him who fears God and the Day of Resurrection, and remembers God frequently," Surah 33:21.

Muhammad's example is difficult to follow. Not because he was not a man – he was, Surah 18:110. Not because he was sinless – in fact, he sinned, Surah 40:55; 48:1-2. It is difficult to follow because Allah made unique provisions and a double standard for Muhammad. According to the revelations that Muhammad recited, he was given special privilege and leeway because he was the prophet of Allah.

Muhammad taught Muslim men that they must limit themselves to four wives, Surah 4:3. Yet Allah allowed Muhammad to have many more wives by special revelation, Surah 33:50-52. "A Muslim defender of Muhammad, writing in *The*

Prophet of Islam as the Ideal Husband, admitted that he had fifteen wives! Yet he told others they could have only four wives."[6]

Also, Muhammad taught Muslims that Allah had revealed a special etiquette for the way they were to treat him and behave themselves in his presence. This did not apply to anyone else. Because he was Allah's prophet, he was to be treated better than the average Muslim man. Because he was Allah's prophet, his wives could never remarry after his death, though other Muslim widows could. Remember, Muslims believe these are purely the words of Allah that Muhammad communicates.

"God and His angels shower their blessings on the Prophet. O believers, you should also send your blessings on him, and salute him with a worthy greeting," Surah 33:56.

"O you who believe, do not enter the house of the Prophet for a meal without awaiting the proper time, unless asked, and enter when you are invited, and depart when you have eaten, and do not stay on talking. This puts the Prophet to inconvenience, and he feels embarrassed before you; but God is not embarrassed in (saying) the truth...It does not behoove you to annoy the prophet of God, or to ever marry his wives after him. This would indeed be serious in the sight of God," Surah 33:53.

Finally, Muhammad taught Muslims to be honest and keep their oaths, Surah 5:105-108. Hypocrites are condemned, Surah 48:6. Yet Allah allowed for Muhammad to break his oaths when it suited him.

> The Qur'an itself informs us that Muhammad was not indisposed to breaking promises when he found it advantageous. He even got a "revelation" to break a long-standing pledge to avoid killing during a sacred month of Arab: "They ask thee Concerning fighting in the Prohibited Month. Say: 'Fighting therein is a grave (offense)'; But graver is it in the sight of God To prevent access To the path of God," 2:217. Again, "God has already ordained For you, (O men), The dissolution of your oaths (In some cases)," 66:2. Rather than consistency, Muhammad's moral life was sometimes characterized by expediency. [7]

As Muhammad relaxed his stance on honesty, Islam developed five situations where Muslims could lie with impunity:

1. To save one's life,
2. To affect a peace or reconciliation,
3. To persuade a woman, and
4. When taking a trip (business transaction) [...]
5. In winning someone to Islam[8]

However, Muhammad drew a hard line on lying to Allah or Allah's Prophet. While Muslims could lie to non-Muslims and other Muslims (in some instances), they better never tell a lie against Muhammad! Wagner quotes the Hadith to prove this double-standard:

Narrated Al-Mughira: "I heard the Prophet saying, ascribing false things to me is not like ascribing false things to anyone else. Whosoever tells a lie against me intentionally then surely let him occupy his seat in Hell-Fire." (Sahih al-Bukhari 2.378 cf. 1.106-108) [9]

The example of Muhammad could be summed up as, "Do as I say, not as I do." This is not much of an example. However, the New Testament apostles, as Jesus Christ before them, had to practice what they preached. Hypocrisy was stringently condemned, Matthew 23. The God of the Bible is not a respecter of persons, so there was no divine favoritism toward them, Acts 10:34; Romans 2:11; Ephesians 6:9.

The Effect of Uninspired Tradition upon the Authority of Apostolic Example

Despite the obvious double standard for Muhammad, Muslims are determined to follow his example as scriptural authority for actions. A second challenge arises to Muslims in this regard: The Qur'an offers little record of the actions and attitudes of Muhammad. To learn of his example, Muslims must study books called the Hadith (a record of the words and deeds of Muhammad), which admit to being uninspired. The Qur'an is inspired and inerrant to Muslims. The Hadith hold incredible authority and sway, but they are not from Allah per se. However, the Hadith "record" every aspect of Muhammad's life, and by them Muslims seek to follow his example.

> The Prophet is caught as it were in the ordinary acts of his life – sleeping, eating, mating, praying, hating, dispensing justice, planning expeditions and revenge against his enemies […] morality derives from the Prophet's actions; the moral is whatever he did. Morality does not determine the Prophet's actions, but his actions determine and define morality. Muhammad's acts were not ordinary acts; they were Allah's own acts. It was in this way and by this logic that Muhammad's opinions became the dogmas of Islam and his personal habits and idiosyncrasies became moral imperatives: Allah's commands for all believers in all ages and climes to follow. [10]

The Hadith is no small work. There are competing works of Hadith. The most authoritative collection was put together by Sahih al-Bukhari (811-876 A.D.). Notice that al-Bukhari lived and created this work over 200 years after Muhammad died. The Arabic-English collection of al-Bukhari's Hadith is 4, 705 pages long and contained in nine volumes.[11] This is but one such Hadith and Muslims contend it is necessary to be familiar with the Hadith material to truly follow Muhammad's example. This body of men's writings is looked upon as authoritative in religious matters.

According to the South African Council of Muslim Theologians, the Hadith/ Sunnah is the sensible explanation of an otherwise ambiguous Qur'an. They explain, "The Holy Qur'an without the Hadith or Sunnah of the Prophet remains unintelligible in certain instances and in view of that, the Holy Qur'an has, in several verses, ordered Muslims to follow the Prophet in all his deeds and sayings. Therefore, if one believes in the Holy Qur'an, there is no alternative but to uphold the Hadith of the Prophet.[12]

Despite their dependence on these written traditions, only a minority of Muslims have directly encountered a book of Hadith. Most often the information is filtered to them by Islamic teachers and oral tradition. [13]

It is troubling that while Allah commands in the Qur'an for Muslims to follow Muhammad's example, they must turn to uninspired writings and traditions in order to submit. Without attacking the honor or integrity of al-Bukhari or any other compiler, the fact remains that they were fallible men collecting and writing down memories and oral traditions that pertained to Muhammad. And these memories and oral traditions, of course, came from other fallible men. If Allah did not inspire it, then it cannot be held with equal weight as the Qur'an; practically, it must be held in equal weight if the Qur'an is to be obeyed. How can this be?

The effect is that it empowers uninspired traditions of men with equal authority as scripture, revelation from deity. This is an incredible break from the Bible. The traditions and writings of men are not necessary to understanding or keeping any of the Bible's dictates. The Scripture itself is sufficient, 2 Timothy 3:16-17; 2 Peter 1:3. Furthermore, to place the traditions of men as equally authoritative to God's word is clearly condemned, Matthew 15:1-9.

The Effect upon the Authority of Mandated Conclusions

What conclusions can be mandated from imperatives that may or may not have been abrogated by contradicting imperatives? The doctrine of abrogation means imperatives cannot be trusted. This is the problem of the Qur'an.

What conclusions are necessitated when drawn from the example of one whom Allah made exceptions for and set a rule apart unto him? Clearly his deeds are not to be followed in every respect, as his words at times contradict them. Should people follow the example of one whose teaching admittedly contradicts his practice? This is the problem with Islam's prophet.

Why can't the "inspired" Qur'an be understood and applied apart from the uninspired writings called the Hadith? Why is Allah's revelation insufficient to direct all of the Muslim's ways? Why does it require men's accounts and reminiscences of Muhammad to make up what is lacking? The uninspired writings of men should not be the basis to necessarily infer doctrine and practice! Only that of divine origin can be trusted in such matters.

Islam offers nothing that would justify making "necessary" inferences as scriptural authority in faith and practice. There is nothing to trust as absolute. Instead, Islam offers contradictory "scripture," a double standard example, and the traditional writings of mortal men.

By What Authority?

There are real differences in Islam and Christianity regarding establishing scriptural authority. Followers of both religions see the need to have scriptural authority in order to act in the favor of God. But where does one turn for it, and how is it ascertained?

Christians turn to the New Testament as the sufficient pattern. Muslims turn to the Qur'an as well as the collection of uninspired men's writings, the Hadith, for their pattern.

Christians know to keep all of the precepts revealed in the New Testament. Muslims must do their best to choose the correct imperatives to obey in the face of contradictory commandments in the Qur'an.

Christians are directed to follow the approved examples of the apostles and the first century church which was under their guidance. Christians were amenable to the same Word then as Christians are today. Muslims are told to follow Muhammad, but it quickly becomes apparent that Muhammad was above the law he recited.

Christians have sound commands and examples to make necessary inferences upon in directing spiritual life. Muslims have no solid ground upon which to stand. The inspired record of example is incomplete, and the precepts are contradictory and abrogated. No conclusion can be true when all its premises are dubious or blatantly false.

Islam makes a break in the quality and sufficiency of scripture from the Bible. The inspired Bible is complete, inerrant, and sufficient. The recitations composing the Qur'an are not. There is no consistency of interpretation between the Bible and the Qur'an. Scriptural authority has been established in the same ways throughout the ages with the Bible, while the Qur'an is unable to indisputably authorize by the same standard. This undercuts the notion that Allah is responsible for both the Bible and the Qur'an. These are not consistent messages from the same voice in any respect.

The question does arise: to what standard is the Muslim amenable?
*   Is it the Bible? The Qur'an says "yes," Surah 2;136.
*   Is it the Qur'an? The Qur'an says "yes," Surah 9:33; 47:2; 33:36.
*   Is it the Hadith? The Qur'an warns of the corruptive influence of men's traditions in the past (Surah 12:111; 31:6) and declares its own superiority to men's traditions, Surah 45:6; 77:50. Yet Muslims find themselves unable to understand and keep the Qur'an apart from certain Hadith.

When such a mixed message is given as to the revelation Allah wants Muslims to follow, can anyone be surprised that Islam lacks a consistent standard to establish scriptural authority? In Islam it is possible for man to do nearly anything in the name of Allah and point to some kind of scripture or tradition to back it up.

Lesson 4 Questions

1. Define the word "pattern."

2. What would the universe be like if the Creator preferred chaos to design and authored confusion instead of order?

3. What does the Bible provide to substantiate its claims to sufficiency?

4. What is the three-fold method of establishing scriptural authority in the Bible?

5. Give some examples of direct commands in the New Testament.

6. Give some examples of approved apostolic examples in the New Testament.

7. Why should Christians respect apostolic authority?

8. If the Bible and Qur'an came from the same God (as Muslims claim), shouldn't they be consistent in sufficiency and in establishing scriptural authority? Why or why not?

9. What can make it difficult for Muslims to obey precepts in the Qur'an?

10. Why is Muhammad's example a tricky one to follow in every respect?

11. Where must Muslims turn to learn Muhammad's example in order to follow it?

12. According to the doctrine of tahrif (lesson 2), uninspired Jewish and Christian writings had a corruptive effect on Scripture. What would prevent uninspired Muslim writings (like the Hadith) from having a corruptive influence upon the Qur'an?

13. If both the Qur'an and the Hadith be true, about how many "Holy Books" would a Muslim need to study and obey in order to get to Paradise?

14. According to the Qur'an, what kind of Islam can be scripturally authorized: inclusive/tolerant or exclusive/militant? How so?

Endnotes

[1] For excellent studies on Biblical authority see the following: Cogdill, Roy E. Walking By Faith. Bowling Green, KY: Guardian of Truth Foundation. ; Jenkins, Ferrell. Biblical Authority: Practical Lessons to Guide the Bible Student in Determining, Understanding and Applying Biblical Authority. Temple Terrace, FL: Florida College Bookstore, 1990. ; King, Dan and Leon Boyd. Responsibility and Authority in the Spiritual Realm. Bowling Green, KY: Guardian of Truth Foundation, 1992. ; Moore, Billy W. A Study of Authority. Adrian, MO: Lakewood Hideaway, Inc., 2000. Baughn, John, Exercising Authority, Summitville, IN, Spiritbuilding, 2005.

[2] Jenkins, Ferrell. Biblical Authority: Practical Lessons to Guide the Bible Student in Determining, Understanding and Applying Biblical Authority. Temple Terrace, FL: Florida College Bookstore, 1990. p. 22.

[3] Roberts, Mark. "What I Would Say to My Muslim Neighbor." If I Had One Opportunity: Urgent Messages For Today. Ed. Daniel W. Petty. Temple Terrace, FL: Florida College Book Store, 2004. p. 98 .

[4] Caner, Ergun Mehmet and Emir Fethi Caner. Unveiling Islam: An Insider's Look at Muslim Life and Beliefs. Grand Rapids, MI: Kregel Publications, 2002. p. 86-87.

[5] Richardson, Don. Secrets of the Koran. Ventura, CA: Regal Books, 2003. p. 58-59.

[6] Geisler, Norman L. and Abdul Saleeb. Answering Islam. Grand Rapids, MI: Baker Books, 1993. p. 171 .

[7] Geisler, p. 175.

[8] Wagner, William. How Islam Plans to Change the World. Grand Rapids, MI: Kregel Publications, 2004. p. 125.

[9] Wagner, p. 125.

[10] Parshall, Phil. Understanding Muslim Teachings and Traditions. Grand Rapids, MI: Baker Books, 2002. p. 12-13. Also, Dr. Khan's English translation of Bukhari's Hadith could be viewed at http://www.usc.edu/dept/MSA/fundamentals/hadithsunnah/bukhari/ accessed on 10/20/04.

[11] Goldmann, David. Islam and the Bible. Chicago, IL: Moody Publishers, 2004. p. 24.

[12] Caner and Caner, p. 96.

[13] Parshall, p. 12.

Lesson 5

Patriarchs: Abraham, Isaac, and... Ishmael?

"This is the sum of the years of Abraham's life which he lived: one hundred and seventy-five years. Then Abraham breathed his last and died in a good old age, an old man and full of years, and was gathered to his people. And his sons Isaac and Ishmael buried him in the cave...," Genesis 25:7-9.

Death of a Patriarch

Funerals often serve as scenes for family reunions. Relatives can be separated (either geographically or relationally) for some time, but when a prominent relative within the family dies, then gaps are bridged and the family unites to mourn. In the case of Abraham's sons, they were estranged from a very young age. Abraham had six sons by a second wife (Genesis 25:1-2), but the discussion of Islam and Christianity is concerned with two older sons: Isaac (born of Abraham's first wife Sarah) and Ishmael (born of Sarah's maid Hagar).

This scene – where Isaac, Ishmael, and Abraham are gathered in one place – is the essence and nearly the extent of the Biblical "origin" of three religions: Judaism, Christianity, and Islam. This is a scene of unity and peace as Ishmael and his younger half-brother Isaac mourn their father. Ishmael is about ninety, and Isaac is seventy-five years old. As is fitting at a funeral, reflection is due upon the dearly-loved departed. This lesson examines the patriarchal father of two sons. Two brothers, who in turn fathered two nations and each nation has put forth its prophet, its "divinely" sent messenger to save the world.

The messengers are Muhammad, the "Seal of the Prophets" (Surah 33:40) and Jesus of Nazareth, whom "God has made both Lord and Christ," Acts 2:36. Only one of these could be the promised descendent of Abraham that would bless all nations, Genesis 12:3; 18:18. Who are the people that ushered in a promised deliverer? Who are the people promised salvation in the eyes of the Living God?

Abraham, the Common Patriarch

Both Islam and Christianity view Abraham as the great patriarch or father with whom God (or Allah) chose to have a unique relationship. Both the Bible and the Qur'an label Abraham as "a friend of God," James 2:23; Surah 4:125. There is significance attached to being a descendant of Abraham. The New Testament vividly portrays how Jews looked upon Abraham as both a physical and spiritual father, John 8:33, 39, 53. They bristled at the suggestion that Jesus, who stood before them, could somehow be greater than Abraham, John 8:56-59.

Christians look upon Abraham as their spiritual example and patriarch as well, Romans 4:1-5, 10-12; James 2:20-24. It should be noted that not all Christians can claim to be physical heirs of Abraham, as they are not a race of people, but rather a body of people composed of all races, Galatians 3:26-28; Colossians 3:10-11. Thus, only spiritually are all Christians Abraham's seed, Galatians 3:29. Jesus of Nazareth, however, was a physical descendant of Abraham, Matthew 1:2; Luke 3:34.

Muslims claim that Abraham was the first Muslim since Adam, the first man of Allah's creation.

"Who will turn away from the creed of Abraham but one dull of soul? We made him the chosen one here in the world, and one of the best in the world to come, (For) when his Lord said to him: "Obey," he replied: "I submit to the Lord of all the worlds," Surah 2:130-131.

Muhammad taught that Abraham is a worthy example for Muslims to follow.

"You have an excellent model in Abraham and those who were with him, when he said to his people: 'We are through with you, and those you worship other than God. We reject you. Enmity and hate have come between you and us for ever, unless you believe in God the One,' – except for what he said to his father: 'I shall ask forgiveness for you, but I have not power to prevail with God for you.' 'O Lord, we place our trust in You, and turn to You in penitence, and to You is our returning," Surah 60:4.

Abraham is the patriarchal prophet of Islam.[1] The Bible declares Abraham as the father of Ishmael, who in turn fathered several tribes, Genesis 25:12-18; 1 Chronicles 1:28-31. These tribes came to be Arabians. But in the Qur'an, Abraham has many notable feats attributed to him, besides being Ishmael's father, which are not found in the Bible. He constructed the holiest site in Islam, the Ka'bah. A particular revelation bears his name: Surah 14 is titled "Abraham." It is also held that Muhammad is a direct descendant of Abraham.

> "The Old Testament records in Genesis 17:20 that Ishmael, the first son of Abraham, was the father of twelve princes, one of whom was Kedar... Now this Kedar is the ancestor of the prophet Mohammad. Ishmael is generally regarded as the father of some Arabian tribes with the descendants of Abraham by a concubine called Keturah."[2]

However, the Qur'an does not contain a genealogy tracing Muhammad's lineage back to Kedar or Abraham.

Abraham in the Bible

Abraham was chosen and called out of his homeland, Ur of the Chaldeans in ancient Mesopotamia, to go to a place that God would show him, Genesis 12:1-9; Acts 7:1-4. Abraham went, not knowing where he was being led (Hebrews 11:8) and three promises were made by God to him:

1. Nation Promise, Genesis 12:2; 15:5. God promised to make Abraham into a great nation. His descendants would be numbered as the stars. Abraham was already seventy-five years old when this promise was initially made to him and he had no children.

2. Land Promise, Genesis 12:7; 15:13-21; Acts 7:5-8. Abraham was told that his descendants – the large nation – would possess all of the land of Canaan, though he was a foreigner there all his days.

3. Seed Promise, Genesis 12:3; 18:18; 22:18; Acts 3:25. Not only would the descendents of Abraham constitute a great nation, but a single descendent would be a blessing, indeed a savior to all the nations – the entire world!

As the Old Testament unfolds, readers see God faithfully (and in His time) keeping these promises made to Abraham. In the days of Moses, it is recognized that God had multiplied the descendants of Abraham into the nation of Israel, thus fulfilling the first promise, Deuteronomy 1:10; 10:22; Nehemiah 9:23. Then in the days of Joshua, the Bible shows that God kept the second promise to Abraham by giving the promised land to his descendents to possess, Deuteronomy 1:8; Joshua 23:14; 24:13; Nehemiah 9:23; Acts 7:45.

It is the New Testament that tells us of the final promise being kept: the seed that would bless all nations. It is Jesus Christ, Acts 3:25; Galatians 3:16. He was the prophesied One, and by His gospel all nations can have the forgiveness of their sins, reconciliation with God, and the salvation of their souls, Romans 1:16; Mark 16:15-16.

Many Sons, But Only One Son of Promise

If Isaac had been an only child, it would not be necessary to examine this aspect of Islam and Christianity. But Abraham had several sons, though only one was the promised son.

Ishmael was born to Abraham because Sarah wanted Abraham to have a child. Sarah was barren, and gave her handmaid Hagar to Abraham that he might have a child by her. This was Sarah's plan, not God's plan, Genesis 16. Ishmael was a son of Abraham, but not the son God had promised or chose for His purposes.

Isaac was born to Abraham because God wanted Abraham to have this son, Genesis 17:19-21. God's intention was for Sarah to have the baby with Abraham all along, Genesis 17:15-19. Isaac was the one who Abraham gave all his wealth to, and Isaac was the one with whom God perpetuated His covenant, Genesis 25:5-6; 26:3-5.

According to Genesis, God was not harsh with Ishmael or Hagar; rather, He promised to make Ishmael into a great nation, and He kept His word, Genesis 16:7-17; 17:20; 21:8-21. However, God repeated the three promises of Abraham to Isaac, demonstrating that Isaac was the one son of promise, and from his seed all nations would be blessed, Genesis 26:3-5.

Abraham in the Qur'an

Abraham is a prominent figure in the Qur'an, but many Bible students would hardly recognize him. The Qur'an speaks of Abraham often, but his account is retold in a way that bears little resemblance to the man of God found in the Bible.

Abraham is an important Qur'anic figure. Muhammad spoke of him often, as Richardson notes: "Actually Mohammed retells aspects of Abraham's story – with Biblical and legendary content intertwined – in 24 of the Koran's first 87 chapters. That is 1 retelling in every 3.6 chapters."[3]

Islam is termed the "Creed of Abraham," Surah 2:130-131. His "conversion" story is told many times, with some variation, but always with the same conclusion: he rejected the idolatry of his father, and his native people, and left.

In the Qur'an, Abraham is a mighty preacher and powerful apologist for Allah against idolatry.

- Abraham was a prophet of Allah, Surah 19:41.
- Abraham won a debate he had with a king over the source of authority and power being Allah and not earthly rulers, Surah 2:258.
- Abraham preached against idols and idolatry, Surah 26:69-82; 29:16-18, 26-27.
- Abraham physically smashed idols that his neighbors worshipped, Surah 21:51-70; 37:85-113.

Not surprisingly, a greater emphasis is placed upon Abraham's relationship with Ishmael in the Qur'an than in the Bible. Some of the words and actions attributed to Abraham in the Qur'an resemble Biblical truth, but most are fantastic and thoroughly unbiblical.

For instance, Abraham nearly sacrifices *Ishmael* to be pleasing to Allah, Surah 37:100-112. As the Qur'an tells it, the test of whether Abraham would kill his only son at Allah's request comes before he receives the good news about Isaac's birth. Obviously, this mimics the Biblical account concerning Abraham and *Isaac,* Genesis 22:2-19. However, the same significance is not placed upon this near sacrifice as in the Bible. Biblically, the Genesis 22 account foreshadows the redemptive work of God, who did not stay His hand, but sacrificed Jesus Christ for the sins of the world, John 3:16. But what does this revised tale mean in the Qur'an? Allah never sacrificed his only son for the world – Allah admits no son, Surah 112.

According to the Qur'an, Abraham built the Ka'bah with Ishmael.[4] If that is true, they must have built it well, for it stood in Muhammad's day and still remains today. **"And when Abraham was raising the plinth of the House with Ishmael, (he prayed): 'Accept this from us, O Lord, for You hear and know everything; And make us submit, O Lord, to Your will, and our progeny a people submissive to You," Surah 2:127-128.**

"Remember, We made the House (of Ka'bah) a place of congregation and safe retreat, and said: 'Make the spot where Abraham stood the place of worship;' and enjoined upon Abraham and Ishmael to keep Our House immaculate for those who shall walk around it and stay in it for contemplation and prayer, and for bowing in adoration," Surah 2:125.

In the Qur'an, Abraham kept Hagar and Ishmael near the Ka'bah in Mecca, Surah 14:35-37. Abraham goes to great efforts to make sure his Arabian descendants are provided for by Allah and kept in the way of Islam. Biblically, Abraham sent Hagar and Ishmael away with bread and water, and God took care of them beyond that, Genesis 21:8-21.

The Qur'an does recognize that Abraham had another son named Isaac, Surah 14:39. Isaac is called an apostle, which means he tried to teach Islam to his descendants the Jews, "the people of the book," Surah 19:49-50; 37:112-113. Little is spoken of him in the Qur'an, especially in comparison to Ishmael.

Ishmael and His Legacy
Though the Bible clearly lays Ishmael's birth upon the initiative of Sarah and not God, God cares for Ishmael and blesses him greatly. God comforts Hagar through the message of an Angel, telling her that her baby will thrive. Consider Genesis 16:10-12:

Then the Angel of the Lord said to her, "I will multiply your descendants exceedingly, so that they shall not be counted for multitude." And the Angel of the Lord said to her:
"Behold, you are with child, And you shall bear a son.
You shall call his name Ishmael, Because the Lord has heard your affliction.
He shall be a wild man; His hand shall be against every man,
And every man's hand against him.
And he shall dwell in the presence of all his brethren."

While God is going to make Ishmael into a nation (Genesis 17:20), it hardly sounds as if Ishmael will have an easy life. He will be a strong, proud, and stubborn man, like a wild donkey (so the KJV renders Genesis 16:12). He will have a warring spirit and violent disposition and his life will be challenged by conflict. But he will be successful by his tenacity, and God will see that his descendants multiply.

Bible students have their first glimpse of Ishmael's contrary disposition when he mocks his baby brother in front of the whole family on a feast day, Genesis 21:8-9. The offense was too much for Sarah to bear, and she sent Hagar and Ishmael packing, much to Abraham's distress, Genesis 21:10-11. God repeats to Abraham that He will make Ishmael into a nation because he is Abraham's son, Genesis 21:12-13. But Ishmael is neither the son of promise nor the son of covenant, Genesis 17:15-21.

Once Hagar and Ishmael are cast out of Abraham's household, little more is said of Ishmael. He dwelt in the wilderness of Paran (a desert-region in the area bridging the Sinai Peninsula and the Arabian Peninsula). He became an archer, and his mother arranged his marriage to an Egyptian woman, Genesis 21:20-21.

God kept His sole promise made to Ishmael, and he fathered a nation. Ishmael lived to be 137 years old and had his twelve princes who multiplied into a nation, Genesis 25:12-18. His descendants settled from Shur (a portion of the Sinai Peninsula and wilderness) to Havilah (a northwestern region of the Arabian Peninsula bordered by the Persian Gulf). Basically, his descendants all lived in northern Arabia. They were Arabs.

Not all Arabs come from Ishmael though. According to Genesis 10:25-32, the family of Joktan (descendants of Shem), settled Arabia generations before Abraham lived. There were also millions of other people who inhabited portions of Arabia before, during, and after Abraham's life such as the Sumerians, Assyrians, Babylonians, and Hittites. None of these were descendants of Abraham.

The Bible does not say that Ishmael is the father of all Arabs, but he is the father of some of the Arab people. He is a physical patriarch of some Arabs. The Biblical portrait of Ishmael does not, however, confer on him any religious significance to the God of Abraham, Isaac, and Jacob. Rather Ishmael is another example of God's faithfulness – by keeping His word concerning Ishmael to Abraham.

In the Qur'an, Ishmael is given high rank, playing significant roles in Allah's spiritual plans:
- Ishmael helped build the Ka'bah, Surah 2:128.
- Ishmael is one of the patriarchs, Surah 2:133, 136; 3:84; 14:39.
- Ishmael was "favored" with prophets like Elisha and Jonah and Lot, Surah 6:86.
- Ishmael was a messenger and a prophet, Surah 4:163-165; 19:54-55.

Clearly, Muhammad recites about an Ishmael who is a spiritual leader. Yet Moses' record in Genesis speaks of Ishmael as successful in the ways of this world, but foreign to the grand scheme of God, and lacking in attributes suiting spiritual maturity and leadership. Where does the Bible commend Ishmael's faith? Is he held as an example of meekness, peacemaking, or sacrifice? Where does the Bible say he sought the word of God, let alone instructed others in it?

Ancient Arabians

In the Bible's record (which mainly unfolds God's scheme for humankind's redemption), only occasional mention of the Ishmaelites or ancient Arabians occurs. When they are mentioned, it seems that as a people they retained the description and disposition that the Angel gave to Ishmael in Genesis 16. They remained in the Arabian Peninsula, a largely desert land, living in tents, Jeremiah 3:2; Isaiah 13:20. They were nomads and Bedouins who survived on trade, and often warred among their own tribes. It was a group of Ishmaelite traders who carried Joseph into Egypt and sold him into slavery there, Genesis 37:25-28. Some tribes could unite long enough to harass or rule other peoples. Ishmaelite raiders attacked Israel in Canaan from time to time. When Gideon judged Israel, he led them to defeat some Ishmaelite enemies, Judges 8:21-26.

Guy Woods paints a vivid description of ancient Arabian life in the 600 years between Jesus and Muhammad:

> The Arab peoples often divided into small tribal entities and separated by modes of living and great distances in the deserts, each often jealous of the other and suspicious of each other's intentions, have engaged in bitter feuds with people of their own race for centuries. Often these differences were hereditary, and the conflicts were carried on generation after generation as the sons perpetuated the antagonisms of their fathers. Their nomadic life was not conducive to permanent local settlements, and the average Bedouin family moved from oasis to oasis with its horses, camels, sheep and goats, living contentedly in tents of mohair [...] They were great traders and their caravans traversed the eastern lands from time immemorial laden with spices, cloths, jewels and other articles of trade so highly prized by oriental lands [...] the Arabs were, for hundreds of years idolaters [...] For 500 years following the close of the apostolic age, their religion was Sabianism, the worship of the sun, the moon and other heavenly bodies with which, strangely enough, they had mingled some Jewish and Christian precepts![5]

Islam Sprang from Ancient Arabian Culture
Islam is first and foremost an Arabian religion.
- Its prophet Muhammad was an Arab, born to the powerful Quraysh tribe in Mecca.
- Its holiest site is the Ka'bah, located in Mecca.
- Its prayers (*Salat*) are made in Arabic and directed toward Mecca five times a day.
- Its pilgrimage (*Hajj* - necessary for salvation) is to Mecca.
- Its sacred text (*Qur'an*) was given in Arabic, and it is contended it can only be truly read and understood in that language, Surah 10:37; 43:3-4.
- Its message was initially for Arabs, those who hadn't rejected Allah's word like "the people of the book," Surah 3:3; 22:78; 12:1-3.
- Its adherents are mainly Arabs, though clearly non-Arabs the world over have converted since the seventh century.

At the height of his influence as prophet and theocratic ruler of Arabia (630-632 A.D.), Muhammad, through the propagation of Islam, had united all the Arabian tribes religiously and nationally. A special revelation addressing the Muslims calls upon Muhammad to recognize this:

"O believers, fear God as He should be feared, and do not die but submitting (to Him). Hold on firmly together to the rope of God, and be not divided among

yourselves, and remember the favours God bestowed on you when you were one another's foe and He reconciled your hearts, and you turned into brethren through His grace, You had stood on the edge of a pit of fire and He saved you from it, thus revealing to you His clear signs that you may find the right way perchance. So let there be a body among you who may call to the good, enjoin what is esteemed and forbid what is odious. They are those who will be successful. So be not like those who became disunited and differed among themselves after clear proofs had come to them. For them is great suffering," Surah 3:102-105.

The Arabian tribes were factious and violent until the days of Muhammad. The unification and mobilization of Arabia as a dominant world force was Muhammad's achievement that would shape world history for 1100 years in Africa, Europe, Asia, and the Middle East.

Some Arabs were "united" by Islam at the point of a sword. An example of this would be the conversion of the city of Mecca in 630 A.D. when Muhammad gathered an army of 10,000 Muslims to attack the city. One day before the army arrived, Mecca surrendered, and the terms of their surrender included conversion. Still, other Arabs converted peacefully to Islam. They found many features of Islam to be familiar to the values and religion of pre-Islamic Arabia.

Muhammad's recitations, constituting the Qur'an, evidently borrowed from existing Arabian traditions and beliefs, incorporating them into the new doctrine of submission. It can be seen that Islam in its infancy reflects many seventh century Bedouin values:

> ...The values of village cultures and their nomadic antecedents left an undeniable impact on Islam; indeed, it may be shown that the values shaped the core of Islamic tenets and supplied the believers with a good many of their mainsprings of action, if not their dynamism. Mobility, the loyalty to family and tribe, hospitality, simple concepts of religion, and aggressiveness are among the principle traits which the nomadic Arab carried over into Islam with him.[6]

Familiar aspects of pre-Islamic Arabian "spirituality" are carried over into Islam as well. They are somewhat revised and retold by Muhammad, but they are no less present. These familiarities would ease the transition for Ishmael's descendants, along with other Arabs, to submission.

1. Islam retains the Ka'bah. As mentioned, this temple in Mecca was the center of Arabian worship. Mecca was a prosperous metropolis, largely because it housed the Ka'bah, and Arabians kept it a place of sanctuary and worship. In Islam, the Ka'bah is cleansed of 359 of its "deities," but it is still the holiest site for the worship of Allah. Muslims must still travel there to worship. The Ka'bah did not become "holy" with Muhammad; its "sanctity" carried over into Islam.

2. Islam retains Superstition. Pre-Islamic Arabs were a very superstitious people. They believed in magic stones, the "evil eye," and fantastic stories about genies or fairies (*jinn*). They practiced casting curses and spells. Morey writes, "It is no surprise therefore to find that the Qur'an also contains references to such things as the evil eye, curses, fatalism, and the fabulous jinns, Surahs 55; 72; 113 and 114. In many Islamic countries, Muslims still wear an amulet around their neck in which a part of the Qur'an is recorded to ward off the 'evil eye'."[7]

3. Islam retains Jewish influences. In seventh century Arabia, Jews were dispersed in many settlements. The town of Medina, where Muhammad grew to be a wealthy political leader as well as a successful military general, had a large and wealthy Jewish population. When Muhammad first arrived in Medina, Allah's revelations promoted aspects of Judaism, such as respecting certain dietary regulations (Muslims do not eat pork or other "unclean" foods) and commanding prayers be directed toward Jerusalem (until that was abrogated and prayers were aimed back to Mecca). The link between Abraham, Ishmael, and Biblical prophets to Muhammad and his movement was stressed in order to build an alliance with the Medinan Jews. However, as Jews refused to convert to Islam, and tensions grew between them and the Arab Muslims, more of Allah's revelations spoke of the Jews' hypocrisy and corruption of Scripture.

4. Islam retains "Christian" influences. Due to the Arabians' successful history of trading, their long routes had brought them in contact with Christian doctrines for 600 years before Muhammad lived. It was a corrupted Christianity that many Arabs of the time knew: that is, Roman Catholicism or Gnosticism. But concepts of the trinity, virgin birth, and the crucifixion and resurrection of Christ had all been planted in Arabia. Some of Allah's revelations spoke highly of Jesus, calling him a great prophet and apostle, though core truths of the gospel were revised or denied.

5. Islam retains the god of gods, Allah. Pre-Islamic Arabians worshipped the moon-god, Allah. They had for centuries when Muhammad came along. Allah was considered the "supreme deity," that is, the prominent deity of the pantheon of pre-Islamic Arabian gods.[8] Ancient Arabia's Allah was the father of goddesses, such as the Arabian deities Al-Lat, Al-Uzza, and Manat. Allah was worshiped at the Ka'bah along with 359 other gods. Muhammad's first recitations dealt with Allah's superiority to idols, and stated that Allah's prominent place among other gods was not sufficient: Allah was to be the sole *God*. Muhammad's revelations clearly broke the pre-Islamic association of Allah and the moon.

"The night and day and the sun and moon are (only) some of His signs. So do not bow before the sun and the moon, but bow in homage to God who created them, if you truly worship Him," Surah 41:37.

The sign of the moon-god Allah was the crescent moon, a symbol carried over into Islam and still prominently displayed atop mosques and on national flags. The crescent moon was not new with Muhammad's visions; Ishmaelites in the Bible wore this unique shape as jewelry, denoting their heritage and worship rituals, Judges 8:21-26. Allah was a familiar name, and his crescent a familiar symbol to recently converted Muslims of seventh century Arabia.[9]

What is Gained from the Study of "Father" Abraham and his Sons?

Christians should see that there are points of reference and discussion with Muslims in the Genesis account. It must be understood that Muslims "know" Abraham, but the Abraham they "know" is presented quite differently in the Qur'an. A study of his life from the Bible, as well as other Old Testament figures that have been revised and their stories retold in the Qur'an, may prove fruitful.

It is also seen that Islam developed much more from the religious milieu of ancient Arabians (including Ishmaelites) than from the teaching or accomplishments of Ishmael himself or his father, Abraham.

Spiritual explorers should see that there is a God and He has a plan. Abraham figures prominently in it. Both of his sons are patriarchs of nations. One is the patriarch of the nation which ushered in the great deliverer. All must decide if it was Ishmael and Islam, or Isaac and ultimately Christianity.

Muslims should see that there is a wealth of information to be gained about the great patriarch Abraham by reading Genesis and other Biblical accounts. He is significant in the Bible, neither for smashing idols nor building a holy temple, but rather for leaving his homeland and traveling to a land that God would show him. He is still a patriarch to spiritual children dwelling in tents and awaiting a city with a foundation, one which God builds, Hebrews 11:8-10.

Lesson 5 Questions

1. How many sons did Abraham have?
2. How many sons were promised to him by God?
3. Who was Abraham's oldest son? Who received Abraham's inheritance?

4. What promises did God make to Abraham and then Isaac?

5. What promise was made concerning Ishmael? Did God keep that promise?

6. What was Ishmael like according to the Bible?

7. How is Abraham different in the Bible and the Qur'an?

8. How is Ishmael different in the Bible and the Qur'an?

9. Are all Arabians descendants of Ishmael?

10. List some instances where Ishmaelites are mentioned in the Bible.

11. What information does the Bible give us about the Ishmaelites?

12. What kind of evidence would be necessary to demonstrate that Muhammad and Ishmael are related?

13. Why would Muhammad want to establish a lineage, linking himself to Abraham?

14. What aspects of pre-Islamic Arabian religion carried over into Islam?

15. List some talking points that this lesson might present in a conversation with a
    Muslim friend or neighbor pertaining to religious matters.

Endnotes

[1] Farah, Caesar. Islam. 6th ed. New York: Barron's, 2000. p.70.

[2] El-Dareer, Dr. Salah. The Hutto-El-Dareer Debate. Indianapolis, IN: Faith and Facts Press. 2004 Reprint of 1974 debate. P. 91.

[3] Richardson, Don. Secrets of the Koran. Ventura, CA: Regal Books, 2003. p. 96.

[4] The word Ka'bah is Arabic for "cube" and refers to the square stone temple in Mecca that is Islam's holiest site. When Muslims make their Pilgrimage, it is to this site, Surah 3:96-97. In Muhammad's day, seventh-century A.D. Arabia, the Ka'bah was the center of idolatry for the Arabian Peninsula with 360 gods represented and worshiped there.

[5] Woods, Guy N. Biblical Backgrounds of the Troubled Middle East. Nashville, TN: Gospel Advocate, 1991. p. 53-54.

[6] Farah, p. 22.

[7] Morey, Robert. The Islamic Invasion. Las Vegas, NV: Christian Scholars Press, 1992 p. 41.

[8] Farah, p. 31.

[9] Morey links extensive scholarship as well as archaeological research to make a compelling case that Muhammad's Allah is a revision of the Arabian moon-god. See especially chapters four and five and Appendix C of The Islamic Invasion. But Caner & Caner stress that Morey's hypothesis would not be a good talking point with most Muslims because the Qur'an does not teach moon-worship in any way.

See Caner, Emir Fethi and Ergun Mehmet Caner. More Than a Prophet: An Insider's Response to Muslim Beliefs About Jesus & Christianity. Grand Rapids, MI: Kregel Publications, 2003. p. 26-27.

Lesson 6

Muhammad: The "Seal of the Prophets"

"Beloved, do not believe every spirit, but test the spirits, whether they are of God; because many false prophets have gone out into the world," 1 John 4:1.

Who is Muhammad?

The daily practice of Muslims is greatly shaped by the life of Islam's prophet Muhammad. Muhammad was a real person of history. Though he has been largely overlooked in educating Western Civilization's youth about world history, his accomplishments in leadership and conquest arguably rival Alexander the Great. Like Alexander, Muhammad managed to unite separated and antagonistic tribes into a force that marched under his leadership and beyond his lifetime to occupy much of the known world. Unlike Alexander, Muhammad is revered by one out of every six people on earth.

"Philosopher, orator, apostle, legislator, conqueror of ideas, restorer of rational dogmas, of a cult without images; the founder of twenty terrestrial empires and of one spiritual empire, that is Muhammad. As regards all standards by which human greatness may be measured, we may well ask, is there any greater than he?"[1] This quotation probably does not go far enough in capturing the Muslim's esteemed view of Muhammad. Most Muslims will not write nor utter his name without saying, "peace be upon him" (pbuh), or something to that effect.

As men count greatness, Muhammad is an example of gaining all this world can offer. However, as the Bible reveals greatness, success is measured by an entirely different standard, Matthew 20:24-28; 1 John 2:15-17; 1 Timothy 6:7-8; Ecclesiastes 12:13-14.

"It may be truly affirmed that of all known legislators and conquerors not one can be named, the history of whose life has been written with greater authenticity and full detail than that of Muhammad."[2] As seen in lesson four, approximately 200 years after his death, stories of Muhammad's life were gathered by uninspired writers and written as Hadith (a record of the words and deeds of Muhammad). The compilers of Hadith did not record every fable they heard about Muhammad, but sought to verify the stories and only retain what could best be substantiated. The bodies of work (for there are multiple Hadiths by different compilers), if respected as historically accurate, record every aspect of the prophet's daily life to the smallest detail.[3]

It is beyond the scope of this study to examine the voluminous Hadiths. The point is that between these and secular history, there is abundant material to search in order to gain a picture of the life of Muhammad. The Qur'an itself is greatly insightful to what Muhammad was all about. First, some biographical information is in order.

Muhammad's Story[4]

Muhammad was born in approximately 570 A.D. in Mecca on the Arabian Peninsula. He died in Medina in 632 A.D. around age sixty-three. His tomb remains in Medina to this day, and is the second holiest site in the religion of Islam after the Ka'bah.

Muhammad was the son of Abdullah and Aminah, members of the ruling tribe of Mecca, the Quraysh. Though the leaders of this tribe were in fact distant relatives and quite wealthy, Muhammad grew up in poverty. His father died before Muhammad's birth, and he was only six when he lost his mother. At that point Muhammad went to live with his grandfather Abu al-Muttalib, an arbiter as well as custodian at the Ka'bah. Muhammad's experiences around this center of pagan worship doubtless had an impact upon his teaching later in life.

Once his grandfather died, Muhammad was entrusted to his uncle, Abu-Talib. Little is known of his childhood except what can be inferred: he experienced poverty (by being orphaned), neglect (wealthy relatives did not relieve him), heartbreak (from the death of caregivers), and pagan indoctrination (from exposure to the Ka'bah).

By age twenty-five, Muhammad was making his way in the world by leading trade caravans. Through such a business endeavor, he met Khadija, a wealthy widow who hired him to lead a caravan for her. Muhammad served her successfully, and after the business venture, the two were married. Muhammad was twenty-five and Khadija was forty. They were married for fifteen years when Khadija died. She bore two sons who died in infancy and four daughters, two of whom married future Caliphs. ("Caliph" was the title of the Islamic leader used after Muhammad's death). As long as Khadija lived, Muhammad took no other wife; after her death, he drank deeply from the well of polygamy.

At age forty, Muhammad was a wealthy and respected businessman. His annual custom was to take a month and go to the caves in the mountains outside of Mecca and meditate. According to Muslim doctrine, in the month known as Ramadan, when Muhammad was forty years old, Gabriel appeared to him in a cave with the first revelation of the Qur'an.

The common tale of Muhammad's first recitation is harrowing.[5] Gabriel surprised Muhammad when he was meditating in the cave. The angel put his hands around Muhammad's throat, choked him, and yelled, "Recite! Recite!" Muhammad gathered enough breath to protest. The violence continued until Muhammad choked out the first words of the Qur'an:

"Read in the name of your Lord who created, Created man from an embryo; Read, for your Lord is most beneficent, Who taught by the pen, Taught man what he did not know," Surah 96:1-5.

Then Gabriel departed.

When Muhammad returned to Khadija from this encounter, he was unsure what the event had meant, and was concerned that a *jinn* (evil spirit) might have overcome him. Khadija communicated with a Christian cousin who assured her that Muhammad's revelations came from the same source that had inspired Moses. And like Moses, Muhammad would be a prophet for his people. [6] At this point (approximately 610 A.D.), Khadija, as well as Muhammad's uncle Abu-Talib, believed in Muhammad's prophetic calling more than he did, and they encouraged him to preach.

Muhammad's ministry in Mecca consisted of proclaiming social justice and equality for the poor while denouncing polytheism. Muhammad quickly adopted the doctrine that Allah was the only god, and it was wrong to worship or serve any other. At first his preaching was barely noticed, but his message of strict monotheism gradually increased in force. The political powers of Mecca began persecuting him and his band of Muslims because they felt his teaching was detrimental to the economy, which flourished from pagan worshippers traveling to the Ka'bah. Muhammad and the Muslims left Mecca for Medina amidst plans of the Quraysh leaders to assassinate him.

In 622 A.D., Muhammad moved to Medina. This journey is called the *Hijrah*. Subsequently, this year became the first year of the Islamic calendar, and marked the beginning of the Islamic era.

Muhammad prospered in Medina. He established himself as an arbiter between feuding Arabian tribes, and as the statesman and ruler of Medina, he united all the factious groups. At this point, everything Muhammad does is in relation to Islam. He must be accepted as the prophet of Allah by all in Medina. When two Jewish clans living in Medina did not accept him as a prophet of God, Muhammad started receiving Surahs that were violent toward dissenters, Jews, and other "People of the book." Two prominent Jewish clans were forcibly cast out of Medina.

It was during these years that Muhammad established himself as a skilled military leader. He led raids against trade caravans that would profit Jews or Meccan Arabs. He engaged the Quraysh-led forces coming from Mecca to stop him. Muhammad's Surahs reveal the doctrine of *jihad* over the years 624 to 630 as he inspired his Muslim troops to fight on and fear nothing of defeat or death.

By 630 A.D., Muhammad had raised an army of 10, 000 Muslims to besiege and conquer Mecca. Mecca surrendered a day before the army arrived, and as terms of their surrender, the city officially converted to Islam. Muhammad entered Mecca without resistance. He chose to forgive his Quraysh enemies instead of executing them. He went straight to the Ka'bah and "cleansed" it, destroying all the idols therein and ending the polytheistic practices of pre-Islamic Arabia. With Medina and Mecca now wholly Muslim, Islam spread quickly throughout the Arabian trade routes. Arab tribes soon fell in line and submitted, being united under the prophet and Islam. The religion proved to be more powerful than tribal differences, and Arabia became a united Muslim force.

After twenty-three years, Muhammad had united the Arabian Peninsula (which had never been done before), "recited" the Qur'an, and was the undisputed theocratic ruler of Arabia. Islam was proclaimed forth by both preachers and the sword.

Through the Surahs, Muhammad makes three claims pertaining to his prophethood that must be examined, 1 John 4:1; 2 Peter 2:1; Ephesians 5:11:
- He claimed to be a divinely appointed messenger.
- He claimed to bring divine revelation.
- He claimed to be foretold in the Bible (We will look at this in Lesson 7).

Was Muhammad a Divinely Appointed Messenger?

Muhammad's Mission
A casual reading of the following Surahs makes it clear that the Qur'an contends Muhammad was chosen and called by Allah to be a prophet. Underlining has been added to the quotations for emphasis.

"**Muhammad is not the father of any man among you, but <u>a messenger</u> of God, and <u>the "Seal of the Prophets"</u>. God has knowledge of everything,**" Surah 33:40.
"**Obey God and <u>the Prophet,</u> and beware. If you turn away, remember, that the duty of Our Apostle is to <u>give you a clear warning,</u>**" Surah 5:92.
"**You have indeed <u>a noble paradigm in the Apostle of God</u> for him who fears God and the Day of Resurrection, and remembers God frequently,**" Surah 33:21.
"<u>**Muhammad is only a messenger; and many a messenger has gone before him**</u>**. So what if he dies or is killed! Will you turn back and go away in haste? But he who turns back and goes away in haste will do no harm to God. But God will reward those who give thanks (and are grateful),**" Surah 3:144.
"**O Prophet, We have sent you as <u>a witness and a bearer of happy tidings</u> and an admonisher, And to call (men) to God by His leave, and as a lamp resplendent,**" Surah 33:45-46.

Notice what Muhammad is and is not, according to the Qur'an. He is not a Messiah or Savior. He is not divine and never claims to be. He does claim to be the chief and final prophet (the "Seal of the Prophets"). Furthermore, Muhammad claims to be a messenger, witness, warner, and an example (paradigm) to follow.

Islam does not make Muhammad into a Christ-figure; rather, Jesus Christ is retold in the religion to be merely an apostle, like Muhammad. The Islamic doctrine that Allah wrote the Bible as well as the Qur'an places Muhammad at the end of a long line of Allah's messengers. When Muhammad moved to Medina, his revelations were designed to persuade people that he was of the same tradition as the Old Testament prophets. Yet it was the Jewish clans there who rejected this notion. While Jews and Christians have scriptural reasons to dispute Muhammad's claim to be a divinely appointed messenger, consider this first: why should one listen to any prophet?

Why Listen to a Prophet?

This is a question of authority. Ultimately, a prophet and his message rest on the authority of God. In the Bible, a prophet faithfully declared God's word, and God always kept His word. In the Qur'an, Muhammad recited Allah's words, which could contradict or abrogate Allah's previous revelations. Bible prophets could rest their case upon the faithfulness of God and His word, Numbers 23:19; Titus 1:2. As a similar claim would be difficult for Muhammad to make, he gave other reasons to listen to him:

1. Muhammad Made Threats. Muhammad used brutality to coerce and force some Jews and Christians of his day to convert to Islam. He threatened, and his threats were not idle.

"Those who offend God and His Prophet will be damned in this world and the next. There is a shameful punishment ready for them," Surah 2:57.

2. Muhammad Used Physical Persecution. He used his military forces as a brute squad against infidels such as Jews and Christians. People would listen and submit to this prophet or die.

"O people of the book, believe in what We have revealed, which confirms what is already with you, before we disfigure your visages and turn your faces about and curse you, as We did with those who had broken the Sabbath; and what God decrees comes to pass," Surah 4:47.

"Fight those people of the book who do not believe in God and the Last Day, who do not prohibit what God and His Apostle have forbidden, nor accept divine law, until all of them pay protective tax in submission," Surah 9:29.

3. Muhammad Simply Assumed That Which Demands Proof. He likened himself to legitimate prophets with whom his contemporaries would be familiar. This made him a prophet by association.

"Do you too, O believers, wish to question your Apostle as Moses was in the past? But he who takes unbelief in exchange for belief only strays from the right path," Surah 2:108.

Tests for Genuine Prophethood

Anyone can claim to be a prophet, a messiah, or the president of the United States. But it does not make it so. Evidence must be offered for others to believe the claim. How else can they respect the authority of the message?

Since Muhammad recognized Moses as a prophet, and even likened himself to Moses (Surah 2:108), Moses' teaching on the tests for genuine prophethood are especially pertinent.

The first test of genuine prophethood is accompanying signs, wonders, or miracles. God did not expect people to blindly follow every man who claimed a vision or message from God. In fact, warning is found in Scripture against false prophets. The God of the Bible always worked miracles, signs, and wonders to confirm the authenticity and identity of His mouthpiece. In the absence of such signs, the self-proclaimed prophet is exposed as a fraud.

"'But the prophet who presumes to speak a word in My name, which I have not commanded him to speak, or who speaks in the name of other gods, that prophet shall die.' And if you say in your heart, 'How shall we know the word which the Lord has not spoken?' -- when a prophet speaks in the name of the Lord, if the thing does not happen or come to pass, that is the thing which the Lord has not spoken; the prophet has spoken it presumptuously; you shall not be afraid of him," Deuteronomy 18:20-22.

If one claims to be a prophet, he shall give a sign or make a prophecy. If it fails, that one is a false prophet. His message is not from God.

It is notable that both Jesus and the apostles passed this test in the New Testament. Their teaching was confirmed with miracles, signs, and wonders by God, John 20:30-31; Acts 2:22; Mark 16:15-20; Hebrews 2:2-4.

Muhammad fails this first test. His Qur'an was not accompanied by miracles, signs, or wonders. While the following quote is lengthy, it is very telling. Read it carefully:

"Do not argue with the people of the book unless in a fair way, apart from those who act wrongly, and say to them: "We believe what has been sent down to us, and we believe what has been sent down to you. Our God and your God is one, and to Him we submit." That is how We have revealed this Book to you; and those to whom We have sent down the Book will believe in it. Only those who are infidels will deny it. You did not read any Scripture before this, nor wrote one with your right hand, or else these dissemblers would have found a cause to doubt it. In fact, in the minds of those who have intelligence these are clear signs. No one denies Our revelations except those who are unjust. For they say: "How is it no signs were sent down to him from his Lord?" Say: "The signs are with God. I am only a warner, plain and simple." Is it not sufficient for them that We have revealed the Book to you which is read out to them? It is indeed a grace and reminder for people who believe," Surah 29:46-51.

The verses state plainly that there were no miracles accompanying Muhammad's ministry.[7] The contention is that the message itself is the miracle and should suffice as proof that he is a legitimate prophet. Yet Moses made it clear that the message was distinct from miracles. Anyone can dream up a message, but God confirms His word with signs. Note what is said of those who do not accept that Muhammad's message is the miracle. They are "infidels;" they lack "intelligence;" they are "dissemblers" (dishonest, false pretense); and they are "unjust." This harsh rhetoric, maligning non-Muslims is no substitute for proof! Likely, only "People of the book" were (and are) aware that God demanded tests to authenticate prophethood.

The second test Moses gave of genuine prophethood is agreement with previous revelation. Because prophets spoke for God – and God speaks truth – nothing a prophet said contradicted or abrogated a previously proven revelation. So, once a prophet worked a sign or miracle, closer attention was to be paid to his message. Was the prophet's word consistent with all that God had said before?

"If there arises among you a prophet or a dreamer of dreams, and he gives you a sign or a wonder, and the sign or the wonder comes to pass, of which he spoke to you, saying, 'Let us go after other gods which you have not known, and let us serve them,' you shall not listen to the words of that prophet or that dreamer of dreams, for the Lord your God is testing you to know whether you love the Lord your God with all your heart and with all your soul. You shall walk after the Lord your God and fear Him, and keep His commandments and obey His voice, and you shall serve Him and hold fast to Him. But that prophet or that dreamer of dreams shall be put to death, because he has spoken in order to turn you away from the Lord your God, who brought you out of the land of Egypt and redeemed you from the house of bondage, to entice you from the way in which the Lord your God commanded you to walk. So you shall put away the evil from your midst," Deuteronomy 13:1-5.

Muhammad blatantly defies the second test of genuine prophethood. There is no intention of keeping the Qur'an consistent with previous proven revelation. Instead, to defend the contradictions, Muhammad claims Jews and Christians interpolated and polluted their Scriptures by the doctrine of *tahrif.* Furthermore, Allah reserves the right to change his mind and word by the doctrine of abrogation.[8]

"We have sent no messenger or apostle before you with whose recitations Satan did not tamper. Yet God abrogates what Satan interpolates; then He confirms His revelations, for God is all-knowing and all-wise. This is in order to make the interpolations of Satan a test for those whose hearts are diseased and hardened: Surely the sinners have gone far in dissent," Surah 22:52-53.

"When we cancel a message (sent to an earlier prophet) or to throw it into oblivion, We replace it with one better or one similar. Do you not know that God has power over all things?" Surah 2:106.

Given Muhammad's failures of Moses' inspired tests for prophethood, we see the "warner" condemned by his own curse:

"But woe to them who fake the Scriptures and say: 'This is from God,' so that they might earn some profit thereby; and woe to them for what they fake, and woe to them for what they earn from it!" Surah 2:79.

Is Muhammad a divinely appointed messenger? This claim cannot be sustained.

Did Muhammad Bring Divine Revelation?

Confirmation, Correction, or Contradiction?
    Muhammad claims to bring a divine revelation. Now, if his prophethood cannot be established, serious doubt is cast on his message. However, his claim of divine influence could not be made any clearer, and it should be investigated.

"This Qur'an is not such (a writ) as could be composed by anyone but God. It confirms what has been revealed before, and is an exposition of (Heaven's) law. Without any doubt it's from the Lord of all the worlds," Surah 10:37.

    Notice that not only is the prophet's message from Allah, but it serves to confirm all previous Scripture. That means it should corroborate and verify the Bible, according to this Surah:

"He has verily revealed to you this Book, in truth and confirmation of the Books revealed before, as indeed He had revealed the Torah and the Gospel," Surah 3:3.

    Remember, in some Surahs the message of Allah is said to be like revelation from the God of the Bible – that is, unchangeable. A prophet with a divine message should be able to easily affirm and confirm previous scripture.

"Such was the law of God among those before you; and you will not find any change in the law of God," Surah 33:62.

    In fact, there are many changes from the Bible to the Qur'an. If the Qur'an be received as an authentic divine revelation, it is a mass of revision, correction, and contradiction over and against the Bible. As Richardson asks, why would Allah desire to confirm something as corrupt as the Bible?

    Consider also that God, if he were really speaking through Mohammed, could have – indeed should have, if it was so – declared that he could not confirm the Jewish and Christian scriptures because they were corrupted. Instead, several dozen times Mohammed declares that the Jewish and Christian scriptures are *confirmed* – not *corrected* – by his Koran. Surely

Allah would not confirm anything that had been corrupted. The simple fact is that Mohammed himself did not regard the Old and New Testaments as corrupted. Muslim apologists are actually correcting Mohammed's misperception concerning them.[9]

We will look closer at Muhammad and the Bible in the next lesson.

Convenient Prophesies

The self-serving nature of some of the Surahs is another reason to doubt Muhammad's claim of bearing a divine message. Ample evidence of selfish prophecies are found in Surah 33 and Surah 66. Are Muslims and non-Muslims to believe that Allah shows such gross favoritism and is party to morally questionable activities? Let us consider some examples from Surah 33:

Islam allows polygamy, though a limitation is placed upon the Muslim man: he can have a maximum of four wives, Surah 4:3. He may have fewer, but he cannot have more; that would be iniquitous. However, Allah allowed Muhammad to have many more than four wives by special revelation.

"We have made lawful for you, O Prophet, wives to whom you have given their dower, and God-given maids and captives you have married, and the daughters of your father's brothers and daughters of your father's sisters, and daughters of your mother's brothers and sisters, who migrated with you; and a believing woman who offers herself to the Prophet if the Prophet desires to marry her. This is a privilege only for you and not the other believers. We know what We have ordained for them about their wives and maids they possess, so that you may be free of blame, for God is forgiving and kind," Surah 33:50.

It is difficult to find exactly how many wives Muhammad had. There are different numbers given. All agree that he had over ten wives, and that the youngest was a girl named Aishah, only six years old when they wed.[10] This is a convenient prophecy with disturbing applications.

Not only is the Muslim man limited to four wives, but he is specifically enjoined to love them equally, Surah 4:3. In practical terms, a Muslim man is to have a fixed rotation of relations with his wives that is not broken, thereby showing no preference for one over another. Allah smiled on Muhammad again, allowing him to go to whatever wife he desired, whenever he desired.

"You may defer the turn of any of your wives you like, and may take any other you desire. There is no harm if you take any of those (whose turn) you had deferred. This would be better as it would gladden their hearts and they will not grieve, and each will be happy with what you have given her. God knows what is in your heart, for He is all-wise and benign," Surah 33:51.

According to Farah, Aishah was the prophet's favorite wife. "In these post-Khadija marriages, he is known to have dearly loved Aishah, daughter of his most trusted companion Abu Bakr, and the only virgin wife he ever married. This fact was recognized by his other wives who gave him permission to consort with her without concern for themselves."[11] But Farah is wrong here. It was not the selfless harem who allowed Muhammad this right, but a revelation from Allah!

As Muhammad's popularity grew, he was constantly bombarded by followers who sought his advice or needed a dispute settled. Some simply wanted to meet him and hear him speak. This became exhausting and tedious at times for Muhammad. Luckily, Allah intervened on the prophet's behalf, allowing him to get some peace without upsetting anyone himself.

"O you who believe, do not enter the house of the Prophet for a meal without awaiting the proper time, unless asked, and enter when you are invited, and depart when you have eaten, and do not stay on talking. This puts the Prophet to inconvenience, and he feels embarrassed before you; but God is not embarrassed in (saying) the truth. And when you ask his wife for something of utility, ask for it from behind the screen. This is for the purity of your hearts and theirs. It does not behoove you to annoy the prophet of God, or to ever marry his wives after him. This would indeed be serious in the sight of God," Surah 33:53.

Clearly all these extra men coming around the house was bothering Muhammad. He wanted the men to stay on the other side of the screen from the wives. And they need not even think about marrying these women after Muhammad's death, because they cannot marry anyone else. These instructions were not for any other Muslim man.

Furthermore, because Muhammad was Allah's prophet, he was to be treated better than other Muslim men.

"God and His angels shower their blessings on the Prophet. O believers, you should also send your blessings on him, and salute him with a worthy greeting," Surah 33:56.

The most dubious of these convenient and self-serving prophecies allowed Muhammad to marry Zaynab, the ex-wife of his adopted son Zaid! As the story goes, initially Zaid and Zaynab desired marriage, but it was frowned upon by the larger community. Zaid, being a freed slave and adopted son, was from a lower social level than Zaynab, who came from a noble family of the Quraysh tribe.[12] At that time, Muhammad favored the match and Allah intervened, declaring that if the prophet says something, his word outweighs tradition or communal biases. Consider the far sweeping authority that the following verse grants Muhammad.

"No believing men and women have any choice in a matter after God and His Apostle have decided it. Whoever disobeys God and His Apostle has clearly

lost the way and gone astray," Surah 33:36.

Zaid and Zaynab were wed. Yet the marriage failed. One wonders why Allah could not have intervened again on their behalf and given them counseling that would have saved their marriage. After all, their marriage was so important to Allah it warranted a revelation.

Zaynab did not stay single long, however. When Allah did intervene again, it was to declare his will that Muhammad take Zaynab as a wife. It was shameful and immoral, given ancient Arabian values, for a father to have his son's wife. Yet, if Allah and his prophet decide it would be right for Muhammad to marry Zaynab, who is to argue?

"When you said to him who had been favoured by God and was favoured by you: 'Keep your wife to yourself and fear God,' you were hiding something God was about to bring to light, for you had fear of men, though you should fear God more. And when Zaid was through with her, We gave her to you in marriage, so that it may not remain a sin for the faithful (to marry) the wives of their adopted sons when they are through with them. God's command is to be fulfilled. There is no constraint on the Prophet in what God has decreed for him. This has been the way of God with (apostles) who have gone before you, - and God's command is a determined act," Surah 33:37-38.

In light of such blatant and despicably self-serving prophecy, it cannot be accepted that Muhammad brought a divine revelation.

What Kind of Prophet Was Muhammad?
The "Seal of the Prophets" cannot honestly prove his claims to be a prophet! Though Muhammad likened himself to Moses and other respected prophets, he failed to meet the Biblical tests for a divinely appointed messenger. Though his mission was to "confirm" the Bible with his divine message, he is constantly contradicting or "correcting" by way of revision. Some of his recitations are immoral and grossly self-serving. So much for the claim of bringing a divine message.

The Bible speaks of a prophet such as this and labels him a *false* prophet, Deuteronomy 13:1-5; 18:20-22; 2 Peter 2; 1 John 4:1.

Examining the Truth

Lesson 6 Questions

1. What kind of character traits might be instilled in a man, given an upbringing like Muhammad's?

2. Give some examples of how Muhammad's life still affects the world.

3. List some titles that Muhammad is given in the Qur'an.

4. Explain the two tests given in Deuteronomy to verify that a prophet was divinely appointed.

    a) Explain how Moses passed the tests.

    b) Explain how Elijah passed the tests.

    c) Explain how Jesus passed the tests.

    d) What would have to be different for Muhammad to pass the tests?

5. Is Allah a respecter of persons?

6. What prophet in the Bible received gratuitous, self-serving prophecies that raised him above the law he gave to others?

7. Was Jesus living above the Law of Moses during His earthly ministry, Matthew 5:17-20?

8. According to the Bible, what kind of prophet makes prophetic claims and fails to prove them?

9. Explain the dangers of following a false prophet or false teacher?

10. According to the Bible, what punishment(s) does God decree upon false prophets?

Endnotes

[1] Lalljee, Yousuf N. <u>Know Your Islam</u>. Elmhurst, NY: Tahrike Tarsile Qur'an Inc., 1999. p. 21.

[2] Lalljee, p. 21.

[3] For helpful study on Hadith, see Parshall, Phil. <u>Understanding Muslim Teachings and Traditions</u>. Grand Rapids, MI: Baker Books, 1994.

[4] Much of this information is taken from Farah, Caesar E. <u>Islam</u>. 6th Ed. New York: Barron's, 2000. pp. 35-58.

[5] As noted in lesson three, the Qur'an actually offers four versions of Muhammad's first call to prophethood. This is a synopsis of the most commonly taught and accepted version.

[6] Mabry, Gene. <u>An Introduction to Islam From a Christian Perspective</u>. Missouri City, TX: www.bibleclassmaterial.com, 2002. p.7.

[7] There is a contradiction on this point between the Qur'an and some Hadith. In the Qur'an, Muhammad contends that there is no miracle or sign except the Qur'an, itself, Surah 2:23-24; 29:46-51. In the traditions gathered 200 or more years after Muhammad's death, it is reported that he worked occasional miracles. For instance, one tradition said he split the moon in half one night in Mecca. Since the Qur'an is accepted as Allah's word (superior to the Hadith), and Muhammad addressed the issue of accompanying signs in the Qur'an's contents, this lesson solely deals with what Muhammad taught concerning accompanying signs in the Qur'an. For more information about the Hadith's teaching on Muhammad and accompanying signs, see Ibrahim, I.A. <u>A Brief Illustrated Guide To Understanding Islam</u>. Houston, TX. Darussalem, 1997. p.36.

[8] This reviews information found in Lesson 2.

[9] Richardson, Don. <u>Secrets of the Koran</u>. Ventura, CA: Regal, 2003. p. 111.

[10] Caner, Emir Fethi and Ergun Mehmet Caner. <u>More Than A Prophet: An Insider's Response to Muslim Beliefs About Jesus & Christianity</u>. Grand Rapids, MI: Kregel Publications, 2003. p. 261.

[11] Farah, p. 68.

[12] Farah, p. 67.

Lesson 7
Muhammad and the Bible

"Knowing this first, that no prophecy of Scripture is of any private interpretation, for prophecy never came by the will of man, but holy men of God spoke as they were moved by the Holy Spirit," 2 Peter 1:20-21.

The Third Claim

The last lesson brought to light that throughout the Qur'an Muhammad made three claims pertaining to his prophethood that must be examined, 1 John 4:1; 2 Peter 2:1; Ephesians 5:11:

- He claimed to be a divinely appointed messenger.
- He claimed to bring divine revelation.
- He claimed to be foretold in the Bible.

It was seen that the first two claims cannot be sustained. But what about the third claim? Was Muhammad foretold in the Bible? Our lesson will address this and other questions pertaining to Muhammad and the Bible.

Muhammad was Directed to the Bible

Should Muhammad or Muslims be in doubt as to Allah's will, they are instructed to go back and reference Jewish and Christian Scriptures. It is hard to reconcile how the same Bible can, at times, be a safeguard from evil, while at other times it is falsehood and error leading people away from Islam.

"If you are in doubt of what We have sent down to you, then ask those who have been reading the Book (for a long time) before you. The truth has indeed come to you from your Lord, so do not be one of those who doubt, And do not be one of those who deny the signs of God, or you will be among the losers," Surah 10:94-95.

"The Qur'an does not regard the Bible as a dead book. Sometimes the Qur'an appeals to the Torah and Gospel as an authority for life and doctrine. These texts lean hard against the idea of abrogation and the charge of corruption."[1] The Qur'an is not even consistent as to whether the Bible should be confirmed or corrected. Remember, Muhammad said he was sent to confirm Holy writ but spent much time revising and "correcting" Biblical accounts!

This Sounds Vaguely Familiar...

As Muhammad fulfilled his ministry of "confirmation," his revelation continuously altered sacred text. Not only do his recitations change the theological significance of the Bible, but he did not so much as "confirm" basic narrative integrity. In other words, he confused names, dates, places, and actions in his versions of Biblical accounts. One reads the following verses of the Qur'an and wonders if people in Muhammad's day heard his distortions of Bible accounts and questioned him about it:

"That your companion is not confused, nor has he gone astray, neither does he speak of his own will. This is only revelation communicated, bestowed on him by the Supreme Intellect, Lord of power and wisdom," Surah 53:2-6.

Clearly, Muhammad stuck to his guns of abrogation. He was only the messenger, and Allah communicated the message whether it was consistent or not. Besides Abraham and Jesus, other well-known Biblical figures and stories were revised and retold in the Qur'an and said to be the *real* story.

"These are the verses of the immaculate Book. We have sent it down as a clear discourse that you may understand. Through the revelation of this Qur'an We narrate the best of histories of which you were unaware before," Surah 12:1-3.

Let's look at just five examples which are representative of this larger body of error.

1. Confusing Identities. In Surah 19:27-28, Muhammad mistakes Miriam, the sister of Moses and Aaron, for Mary, the virgin mother of Jesus.

"Then she brought the child to her people. They exclaimed: 'O Mary, you have done a most astonishing thing! O sister of Aaron, your father was not a wicked person, nor your mother sinful!'" Surah 19:27-28.

2. Confusing People, Places and Time. In Surah 28:36-38, Muhammad recounts Moses giving signs before Pharaoh to prompt the Exodus. But Haman is mentioned as a servant of Pharaoh's Egypt – actually Haman served in the Persian Empire, Esther 3:1-7:10. In Muhammad's revision, Pharaoh commanded a tower be built to reach to heaven – similar to the Tower of Babel that predated Moses by centuries, Genesis 11:1-9.

"The Pharaoh said: 'O nobles, I am not aware of any other lord of yours but myself. So, O Haman, fire some clay (bricks) to build a tower for me that I may mount up (and see) the God of Moses; for I think he is a liar,'" Surah 28:38.

3. Noah's Flood. At least two outrageous changes are made in Muhammad's revision of this well known account from Genesis, Surah 11:41-43. First, one of Noah's sons did not board the ark, and though Noah entreated him to enter, he stayed outside and drowned. Then Allah revealed that Noah's wife was a harlot, and the son that drowned was by another man. Noah's wife is consequently condemned to Hell, Surah 11:45-47; 66:10. The Bible declares that Noah saved his whole household in the ark, Genesis 6:18; Hebrews 11:7; 1 Peter 3:20-21. Furthermore, Noah's wife is never maligned in the Old or New Testament.

> "And (Noah) said: 'Embark. In the name of God be its course and mooring. My Lord is surely forgiving and kind.' It sailed on waves like mountains (high), and Noah called to his son who was separated from him: 'Embark with us, O my son, and be not one of those who do not believe.' 'I shall go up a mountain,' he said, 'which will keep me from the water.' [...] And a wave came between them, and he was among those who were drowned," Surah 11:41-43.

4.   **The Exodus without a Passover.** Richardson accurately explains that for all the Surahs devoted to recounting the Exodus narrative, the most important part is always omitted.

> If the first 89 chapters of the Koran [...] offer any clues to the content of Mohammed's early revelations, he probably treated the Jews in Medina to a narration he surely felt would spellbind them: the Exodus story! The Koran would later feature Mohammed's renditions of Moses' confrontation with the pharaoh [...] 27 times in his first 89 chapters. In other words, Mohammed repeated that same story once every 3.3 chapters! It surely must have been one of his favorite pulpit pieces. Alas, not even *once* in 27 tellings of the Exodus saga did Mohammed include *the* most integral component of the story: *the Passover!* How could the Jews accept as a prophet a man who – if he even knew about the Passover – had no sense of its importance?[2]

5.   **Pharaoh's Fate.** As Muhammad tells his version of the Exodus story in Surah 17:103 and Surah 26:66, Pharaoh drowned along with his soldiers. The Bible teaches that Pharaoh and his army were destroyed by God in the Red Sea, Exodus 14:8-31; 15:4-5; Hebrews 11:29. It would seem the Qur'an and the Bible are in agreement; then Muhammad's story changes in Surah 10:90-92: at the last moment Pharaoh confesses Allah and becomes a Muslim. In this Surah, Allah saves his life as a lesson for future generations.

> "And we brought the people of Israel across the sea, but the Pharaoh and his army pursued them wickedly and maliciously till he was on the point of drowning, and he said: 'I believe that there is no god but He in whom the people of Israel believe, and I submit to Him.' 'Yes, now' (was the answer), 'though before this you were disobedient and rebellious. We shall preserve your body today that you may be a lesson for those who come after you; as many a man is heedless of Our signs,'" Surah 10:90-92.

To fair minds, Muhammad's inability to confirm previous Scripture, coupled with his propensity to contradict himself, points to the fact that his message was less than divine. How do Muslims handle Muhammad's blatant alterations of Biblical accounts? Farah's assessment, both of Muhammad's lack of scriptural knowledge and his persecution of Medinan Jews, makes the prophet's course sound almost reasonable… almost, but not quite. If Farah is correct, Muhammad was not inspired, and the Qur'an is not "uncreated:"

> The inconclusive manner in which these narratives survive in the Qur'an, moreover, often in vague and sometimes in erroneous confusion, for example where Muhammad mistakes Miriam, Moses' sister for Mary, Jesus' mother, suggests that he derived his knowledge of these accounts and personalities either from uninformed sources or from informants, perhaps Monophysite Christians, whose views of their religion did not comport with the orthodox version of the same […] Although his knowledge of the scriptures was not as deep as that of the experts, it enabled him, at least to his own satisfaction, to meet the criticism of his Jewish adversaries in Medina; criticism which lapsed so strongly into derision that he could eliminate it only by uprooting the Jews from the city and its environs.[3]

Was Muhammad Foretold in the Bible?

According to the Qur'an, Allah authored the Bible and prophesied Muhammad's appearance in its pages.

"Who follow the messenger, the gentile Prophet, described in the Torah and the Gospel, who bids things noble and forbids things vile, makes lawful what is clean, and prohibits what is foul, who relieves them of their burdens, and the yoke that lies upon them," Surah 7:157.

But this revelation cannot be confirmed – even by the Qur'an. It is clear that Muhammad desired to be on a par with the Biblical prophets (as he perceived what that role was), but no scripture was given as evidence for the claim. Muhammad even said Jesus foretold his coming.

"And when Jesus, son of Mary, said: 'O children of Israel, I am sent to you by God to confirm the Torah (sent) before me, and to give you good tidings of an apostle who will come after me, whose name is Ahmad (the praised one),'" Surah 61:6.

Yet the Qur'an fails to quote from the New Testament or the Old Testament in order to demonstrate the scriptures Muhammad fulfilled. Muhammad does not give book, chapter, and verse for the scripture that foretells his coming.

This leaves Muslim apologists with the difficult task of searching the Bible themselves to supply the scriptures that Muhammad failed to mention. In order to do this, Muslim apologists must attack the credibility of the Bible and force Muhammad into its pages. They allege that Jews and Christians have corrupted and interpolated the Scriptures, obscuring Muhammad from clear view. This strategy is self-defeating in two respects:

First, it underscores Allah's indifference or inability to safeguard the integrity of his own revelation. Second, if the Bible is so badly compromised, why should anyone believe that the portions the apologists claim to be true are indeed trustworthy? What special insight or inspiration has the Muslim apologist been given to discern truth from error?

A Muslim Apologist's Argument

Dr. Jamal Badawi is a professor at Saint Mary's University in Halifax, Nova Scotia, Canada, where he teaches in the Departments of Religious Studies and Management. Badawi is a significant Muslim apologist who has written extensively and debated to defend Islam and assert its superiority over Christianity.[4] In his article, "Muhammad in the Bible," he undertakes the challenge of proving Surah 7:157. This work is an excellent example of the lengths Muslims must go to find their prophet on the pages of Holy Writ.[5] Let's look at where his article finds Muhammad in both the Old and New Testaments.

Among other Old Testament texts, Badawi focuses on the messianic prophecy found in Deuteronomy 18:18.

"I will raise up for them a Prophet like you from among their brethren, and will put My words in His mouth, and He shall speak to them all that I command Him. And it shall be that whoever will not hear My words, which He speaks in My name, I will require it of him," Deuteronomy 18:18-19.

Badawi states:

In **Deuteronomy 18:18**, Moses spoke of the prophet to be sent by God who is:

1) From among the Israelite's "brethren," a reference to their Ishmaelite cousins as Ishmael was the other son of Abraham who was explicitly promised to become a "great nation."

2) A prophet like unto Moses. There were hardly any two prophets who were so much alike as Moses and **Muhammad**. Both were given comprehensive law code of life, both encountered their enemies and were victors in miraculous ways, both were accepted as prophets/statesmen and both migrated following conspiracies to assassinate them. Analogies between Moses and Jesus overlooks not only the above similarities but other crucial ones as well (e.g. the natural birth, family life and death of Moses and **Muhammad** but not of Jesus, who was regarded by His followers as the Son of God and not exclusively a messenger of God, as Moses and **Muhammad** were and as Muslims believe Jesus was).[6]

As to the first point, there is no reason to assume that "brethren" refers to Ishmaelites. Why would "brethren" mean an entirely different nationality? Ishmaelites were not Israel's "brethren;" they were gentiles. Gentiles were not brethren. They were unclean! There is no way that Jews would read Deuteronomy 18:18-19 and look to the Ishmaelites or any other gentile nation to produce the prophet. In context, God said this prophet would come from their "midst." *"The Lord your God will raise up for you a Prophet like me from your midst, from your brethren...,"* Deuteronomy 18:15. "Brethren" simply means that the prophet would come from one of the twelve tribes of Israel. In fact, Jesus' earthly lineage was of the tribe of Judah, Hebrews 7:14.

In response to the second point, a very superficial comparison is made likening Muhammad to Moses as the fulfillment of this prophecy. We must understand the full weight of being "a prophet like unto Moses."

"But since then there has not arisen in Israel a prophet like Moses, whom the Lord knew face to face, in all the signs and wonders which the Lord sent him to do in the land of Egypt, before Pharaoh, before all his servants, and in all his land, and by all that mighty power and all the great terror which Moses performed in the sight of all Israel," Deuteronomy 34:10-12.

No other prophet knew God "face to face." Jesus Christ, as God in flesh, uniquely meets this qualification of being "like unto Moses." He existed with God, as God (John 1:1-4; 6:46); spoke with God (Acts 2:34-35; Genesis 1:26; John 12:27-33); and made God known as no other has or could, John 1:14, 18; Philippians 2:5-11; 1 John 4:9. Furthermore, Jesus worked mighty signs and miracles publicly, that is "in the sight of all Israel," Matthew 4:23-25; 9:4-8; 14:18-21; John 20:30-31; Acts 2:22-24. Recall by examining the Qur'an, Muhammad did no miracles and offered no signs.

Moses and Jesus compare much more favorably than Badawi suggests. Both Moses and Jesus were of the twelve tribes of Israel. Both worked miracles in full public view, and both revealed a "comprehensive law code of life." The apostle Peter explained that Moses was speaking directly about Jesus Christ in Deuteronomy 18:18-19 (Acts 3:19-26). Furthermore, multitudes of Jesus' Jewish contemporaries believed He was the fulfillment of Moses' prophecy, John 6:14; 7:40. If Muslim apologists challenge the authenticity of the New Testament significance of Deuteronomy 18:18-19, they only work to discredit the very material that they claim foretells Muhammad, Surah 7:157.

Also, admitting that Jesus is more than a prophet does not diminish His prophethood:

Our Lord has three offices: that of prophet, priest, and king. When He ministered here on earth, He declared God's Word as prophet and by the inspiration of His Spirit has caused it to be written down for our learning. He intercedes for His people as the high priest in heaven, and He also sits on the throne and reigns as King, working out His purposes in this world, 1 Corinthians 15:25; Ephesians 1:18-23.[7]

Badawi next moves to the New Testament and claims Muhammad is foretold during the Last Supper. Jesus tells the twelve – minus Judas Iscariot – that a helper will be sent to them, John 14, 15, 16. Though the *Paraclete* is identified as the Holy Spirit (John 14:26), Badawi contends that the "helper" could be Muhammad.

> In the Gospel according to **John (Chapters 14, 15, 16)** Jesus spoke of the "Paraclete" or comforter who will come after him, who will be sent by the Father as another Paraclete, who will teach new things which the contemporaries of Jesus could not bear. While the Paraclete is described as the spirit of truth, (whose meaning resemble **Muhammad's** famous title Al-Amin, the trustworthy), he is identified in one verse as the Holy Ghost, **John 14:26**. Such a designation is however inconsistent with the profile of that Paraclete. In the words of the **Dictionary of the Bible**, (Ed. J. Mackenzie) "These items, it must be admitted do not give an entirely coherent picture..."

> It was **Prophet Muhammad** (peace be upon him) who was the Paraclete, Comforter, helper, admonisher sent by God after Jesus. He testified of Jesus, taught new things which could not be borne at Jesus' time, he spoke what he heard (revelation), he dwells with the believers (through his well-preserved teachings). Such teachings will remain forever because he was the last messenger of God, **the only Universal Messenger to unite the whole of humanity under God and on the path of PRESERVED truth**. He told of many things to come which "came to pass" in the minutest detail meeting, the criterion given by Moses to distinguish between the true prophet and the false prophets, **Deuteronomy 18:22**. He did reprove the world of sin, of righteousness and of judgement, **John 16:8-11**.[8]

Badawi's article rejects that the *Paraclete* is the Holy Spirit, John 14:26. He writes, "such a designation is however inconsistent with the profile of that Paraclete." Why? Is Muhammad *consistent* with the "profile of that Paraclete"? To answer this, first a clear profile of the *Paraclete* is needed. Whom would he help and comfort? To whom would he remind and reveal truth? The answer is obvious: Jesus is speaking to His apostles, and thus making these promises to His apostles.

1. Read John 14:16 - The *Paraclete* would be with the apostles forever, yet Muhammad was never with the twelve. In fact, he did not live until 500 years after the apostles had all died.

2. Read John 14:17 – The world cannot receive the *Paraclete,* yet Muhammad was a man living in the world. The world saw him. For a time he was rejected in Mecca, but eventually the entire Arabian Peninsula received him. The Spirit of truth would dwell in the apostles. Muhammad certainly did not dwell in the apostles!

3. Read John 14:26 – The *Paraclete* is sent in Jesus Christ's name, yet Muhammad comes in Allah's name, and Allah has no equal and no son. Furthermore, the *Paraclete* will remind the apostles of all that Jesus taught. Muhammad was not

present to remind them of anything. When Muhammad did live he said he brought the words of Allah, not Jesus Christ.

4. Read John 15:26-27 – The *Paraclete* **and** the apostles would "bear witness" of Jesus Christ, yet Muhammad and the apostles offer completely *different* testimony concerning the Savior. The apostles testified that Jesus was the resurrected Lord, the Son of God, Matthew 16:16; Acts 2:22-24, 36. Muhammad denied that Jesus was even crucified, let alone resurrected, and insists that Allah has no son, Surah 4:156-158; Surah 19:35-36.

5. Read John 16:7-9 –The *Paraclete* would convict the world of sin. The sin is identified: **disbelief** in Jesus Christ. Conversely, Muhammad taught that to believe in Jesus Christ is the greatest sin against Allah that one could commit, Surah 9:30! A soul will be damned for believing such a thing, according to the Qur'an.

"The Christians say: 'Christ is the son of God.' That is what they say with their tongues following assertions made by unbelievers before them. May they be damned by God: How perverse are they!" Surah 9:30.

To assert that Muhammad is the *Paraclete* of John 14, 15, 16 goes against both the Bible and the Qur'an. Clearly, these passages do not prophesy Muhammad.

He's Just Not There

Like Badawi, many Muslim apologists have asserted multiple passages from the Old and New Testaments to try and prove the Qur'anic claim of Surah 7:157. They fail again and again.

Most Muslim apologists will take Biblical passages from their contexts in order to make a point. In such manner, the Bible can be used to prove anything. Often they will isolate Hebrew or Greek words and build elaborate theories around their phonetic likeness to Arabic terms of different meaning. Fundamentally, they will attack the integrity of the Bible, claiming perversion by Jews and Christians throughout the centuries. If this is not overtly done, they will attack the notion that the Bible can be read, understood, and trusted by the common man simply for what it says. At times, they offer textual criticism taken from liberal theologians and suggest that "learned" Christians do not trust the Bible.

It is the Muslim apologists' difficult task to undertake, because the Bible simply does not foretell Muhammad, despite the Qur'an's claim to the contrary.

Lesson 7 Questions

1. List some contradictions between Biblical accounts and Qur'anic versions of the same events.

2. How does Dr. Farah explain Muhammad's inability to keep the facts of the Bible stories straight?

3. If Dr. Farah is correct, what impact does his theory have on the following Islamic beliefs? a) Muhammad was an inspired prophet.

   b) The Qur'an is uncreated and infallible.

4. What verses in the Qur'an claim that Muhammad was foretold in the Bible?

5. What verse in the Bible clearly mentions or prophesies Muhammad's arrival or ministry?

6. What common strategies do Muslim apologists employ to assert Muhammad was foretold in the Bible?

7. Does it seem reasonable to teach that the Bible is corrupted, but then use it to prove Muhammad is a true prophet? Explain.

8. Why would Allah charge Muhammad with "confirming" a corrupt revelation?

9. Explain why "The Prophet" of Deuteronomy 18:18-19 could not be Muhammad.

10. Explain why the Helper (*Paraclete*) of John 14, 15, 16 could not be Muhammad.

Endnotes

¹ Saal, William J. <u>Reaching Muslims for Christ</u>. Chicago, IL: Moody Press, 1993. p. 88. He cites portions of Surah 5:44-68 and Surah 10:95 as evidence.

² Richardson, Don. <u>Secrets of the Koran</u>. Ventura, CA: Regal Books, 2003. p. 33. Emphasis his.

³ Farah, Caesar E. <u>Islam</u>. 6ᵗʰ ed. New York: Barron's, 2000. p. 85.

⁴ Mark Roberts, Christian, debated Dr. Jamal Badawi at Lamar University, Beaumont, TX on November 3, 1994. Proposition: "The Bible Teaches Jesus Is Deity." Roberts affirmed and Badawi denied. Contact Westside church of Christ in Irving, TX for more information. www.justchristians.com

⁵ Badawi, Jamal. "Muhammad In The Bible." http://www.islamicity.com/Mosque/Muhammad_Bible.HTM. Downloaded 11/1/04.

⁶ Badawi, p. 2.

⁷ Wiersbe, Warren W. <u>Be Equipped</u>. Colorado Springs, CO: Chariot Victor Publishing, 1999. p. 95.

⁸ Badawi, p. 3.

Lesson 8
Jesus Christ: Stumbling Block

"Therefore, to you who believe, He is precious; but to those who are disobedient, 'The stone which the builders rejected Has become the chief cornerstone,' and 'A stone of stumbling And a rock of offense.' They stumble, being disobedient to the word, to which they also were appointed," 1 Peter 2:7-8.

What To Do With Jesus?

One cannot read the Bible and the Qur'an without discovering that Jesus is a central figure in both Islam and Christianity. Islam does not call for absolute faith and allegiance to Jesus as Christianity does. However, many Christians would probably be surprised to learn just how highly most Muslims view Jesus. The Islamic reverence toward Jesus stems directly from Qur'anic doctrine. Interestingly, Jesus is at once the source of common ground for dialogue among disciples and Muslims, yet at the same time He remains the source of an insurmountable barrier between the two religions.

Jesus is a common figure for Christians and Muslims in the same sense that Abraham, Noah, and Moses are. That is, the Qur'an completely revises their accounts, neglecting or castigating the Bible versions and asserting its own fiction as superior. Muslims who read the Qur'an think they truly know Bible people and Bible stories. In truth, little more than their names are the same!

Muslims are taught that when differences exist between the Qur'an's version and the Biblical account, the Bible is the polluted and inferior Book. There are significant differences between the Qur'an and the Bible when it comes to Jesus. That is why He is a key barrier separating Christianity and Islam. This lesson examines the Qur'an's teaching and Muslim belief about Jesus in contrast with the Biblical Jesus. Upon this important study, one may find himself asking, as Pontius Pilate did so long ago, "What then shall I do with Jesus who is called Christ?" Matthew 27:22.

Amazing Titles: Messiah, Christ

The Qur'an uses titles for Jesus that are familiar to Christians.

- Jesus is called Messiah, Surah 3:45; 4:171; 5:17.
- Jesus is called Christ, Surah 4:157, 172; 5:72, 75; 9:30, 31.

Muslims believe Jesus was the "anointed one." That is, anointed by Allah as a special apostle to Israel to call them to repentance and Islam. They deny He was anointed as the Son of God and humanity's Savior.

Actually, these titles seem inappropriate for the Jesus found in the Qur'an. It is unclear what He was uniquely chosen to do by Allah. Why should He be the Anointed One – the Messiah? What was so special about Him? According to the Qur'an, He was simply one of a long line of prophets Allah unsuccessfully used to reason with the Israelites.

"The Christ, son of Mary, was but an apostle, and many apostles had (come and) gone before him," Surah 5:75.

In the Qur'an, Jesus was no greater than Moses or Noah. He was not even the final or definitive prophet – that was Muhammad's place as "Seal of the Prophets"! There is nothing about the "ministry" of Christ in Islam that was unique, so what exactly was He anointed to do?

In the New Testament, Jesus was confessed as the Christ by Simon Peter, and He blessed Peter for saying it, Matthew 16:16-18. Again, Jesus professed to be the Christ to a Samaritan woman who spoke with Him, John 4:25-26. Nelson's Bible Dictionary succinctly states the significance of being the one and only Christ:

> CHRIST (anointed one) - a name for Jesus which showed that He was the long-awaited king and deliverer. For centuries the Jewish people had looked for a prophesied Messiah, a deliverer who would usher in a kingdom of peace and prosperity, Psalm 110; Isaiah 32:1-8; Amos 9:13. Jesus was clearly identified as this Messiah in Peter's great confession, "You are the Christ, the Son of the living God," Matthew 16:16.[1]

Jesus was anointed by the Holy Spirit following His immersion by John the Baptizer, Matthew 3:13-17; Mark 1:9-11; John 1:32-34; Matthew 12:15-18. He was the fulfillment of centuries of Old Testament prophesies concerning a chosen deliverer for Israel. In fact, Jesus was the Savior of the world. He said the Scriptures testified of Him, and it is clearly seen what He was anointed to do. In Nazareth, He publicly read from Isaiah concerning His Messiahship.

"The Spirit of the Lord is upon Me,
Because He has anointed Me to preach the gospel to the poor.
He has sent Me to heal the brokenhearted,
To preach deliverance to the captives
And recovery of sight to the blind,
To set at liberty those who are oppressed,
To preach the acceptable year of the Lord."

Then He closed the book, and gave it back to the attendant and sat down. And the eyes of all who were in the synagogue were fixed on Him. And He began to say to them, "Today this Scripture is fulfilled in your hearing," Luke 4:18-21.

The Messiah came to seek and save that which was lost, Luke 19:10. He was the atoning sacrifice for the sins of the world, John 1:29; Matthew 20:28; 26:28. He held the office of prophet, priest, and king. In the Old Testament, these were anointed positions. Elisha was anointed by Elijah to succeed him as prophet of Israel, 1 Kings 19:16. The Levitical high priest was anointed to serve God, Exodus 28:41; 29:7; 30:30; Leviticus 4:3; 6:22; 7:36. The king of Israel was anointed in order to lead God's people, 1 Samuel 10:1; 16:13; 1 Kings 1:13; 19:15. The Bible teaches Jesus was anointed to fill all these roles, Hebrews 1:1, 8-9; 7. While the Qur'an offers a long list of equals to the Christ – and even a superior prophet – the Bible teaches that Jesus Christ is peerless – the Messiah!

While Jesus is called Messiah and Christ in the Qur'an, these are empty words. In Islam, the full weight of Messiahship is not respected. Jesus is not the believer's high priest, nor is He the reigning king of a spiritual kingdom. And perhaps most importantly, He is not the savior of Jews and Gentiles. Jesus is merely a prophet.

So why would Muhammad call Jesus "Christ" or "Messiah" in the new religion of the seventh century? It would preemptively undercut opposition led by his Arabian Catholic contemporaries (or adherents to other adulterated forms of Christianity of the day), who did not understand the full import of the office of the Christ, but nevertheless insisted Jesus must be the Christ.

Islam's undoing may be in admitting Jesus is Messiah and Christ repeatedly in the Qur'an. For those who care to investigate the significance of the title, it is obvious that Jesus, as the Messiah of Scripture, is much more than a prophet.

Recreated in the Image of Muhammad

For Muhammad to legitimately be viewed as the "Seal of the Prophets" – the greatest and final messenger of Allah – he must tell of a Jesus very different from the one revealed in the Bible. In fact, once Muhammad is done "confirming" all that the Gospels say of Jesus, amazing similarities can be seen between Christ and Allah's favored prophet.

Let's look at five examples of the Jesus found in the Qur'an.

1. Allah sent Jesus as an apostle with a revelation.

"Remember We gave Moses the Book and sent after him many an apostle; and to Jesus, son of Mary, We gave clear evidence of the truth, reinforcing him with divine grace," Surah 2:87.

Likewise, Allah sent Muhammad as an apostle with a revelation.

"O people of the book, Our Apostle has come to you, announcing many things of the Scriptures that you have suppressed, passing over some others. To you has come light and a clear book from God," Surah 5:15.

"These are the messages of God. We recited them to you in all truth, as indeed you are one of the apostles," Surah 2:252.

2. Jesus was inspired with a new revelation that confirmed the previous revelations.

"Later, in the train (of the prophets), We sent Jesus, son of Mary, confirming the Torah which had been (sent down) before him, and gave him the Gospel containing guidance and light, which corroborated the earlier Torah, a guidance and warning for those who preserve themselves from evil and follow the straight path," Surah 5:46.

"And when Jesus, son of Mary, said: 'O children of Israel, I am sent to you by God to confirm the Torah (sent) before me, and to give you good tidings of an apostle who will come after me, whose name is Ahmad (the praised one)...,'" Surah 61:6.

Again, Muhammad's Qur'an was a new revelation meant to merely confirm all previous Scripture.

"And to you We have revealed the Book containing the truth, confirming the earlier revelations, and preserving them (from change and corruption)," Surah 5:48.

"He has verily revealed to you this Book in truth and confirmation of the Books revealed before, as indeed He had revealed the Torah and the Gospel," Surah 3:3.

3. Jesus was an exalted prophet, receiving special notice and treatment.

"Of all these apostles We have favoured some over the others. God has addressed some of them, and the stations of some have been exalted over the others. And to Jesus, son of Mary, We gave tokens, and reinforced him with divine grace," Surah 2:253.

"(Jesus) was only a creature whom We favoured and made an example for the children of Israel," Surah 43:59.

Muhammad was also to be favored and exalted. Much was shown in lesson six demonstrating Allah's favoritism as well as the self-serving nature of portions of Muhammad's "revelation."

"God and His angels shower their blessings on the Prophet. O believers, you should also send your blessings on him, and salute him with a worthy greeting," Surah 33:56.

4. Jesus asked for help to prevail over enemies. While the following verse is vague about the context of their conquest, it is stated that the followers of Jesus did indeed prevail.

"O you who believe, be helpers of God, as Jesus, son of Mary, had said to the disciples: 'Who will help me in the way of God'? and they had answered: 'We are the helpers of God.' Then a section among the children of Israel believed, but a section among them did not. So We helped those who believed against their enemies, and they prevailed over them," Surah 61:14.

Muhammad was not shy either about asking Muslims to assist him in prevailing over his opposition in the most violent terms. Among those whom Muhammad prevailed against were Jews and Christians.

"So, when you clash with the unbelievers, smite their necks until you overpower them, then hold them in bondage. Then either free them graciously or after taking a ransom, until war shall have come to an end. If God had pleased He could have punished them (Himself), but He wills to test some of you through some others. He will not allow the deeds of those who are killed in the cause of God to go to waste," Surah 47:4.

"Fight those people of the book who do not believe in God and the Last Day, who do not prohibit what God and His Apostle have forbidden, nor accept divine law, until all of them pay protective tax in submission," Surah 9:29.

5. Jesus cursed disbelievers.

"Cursed were disbelievers among the children of Israel by David and Jesus, son of Mary, because they rebelled and transgressed the bounds," Surah 5:78.

Muhammad cursed all who disbelieved in him or the tenants of Islam he set forth.

"Those who offend God and His Prophet will be damned in this world and the next. There is a shameful punishment ready for them," Surah 33:57.

"The Christians say: 'Christ is the Son of God.' That is what they say with their tongues following assertions made by unbelievers before them. May they be damned by God: How perverse are they!" Surah 9:30.

These are just some points of comparison made by Muhammad in the Qur'an. They demonstrate that Muhammad retold Jesus in such a way so as to make Jesus a type and shadow of Muhammad himself. By addition and revision of the Biblical Jesus, Muhammad makes it plausible to Muslims that he could be of the same prophethood as Christ – indeed the superior "Seal of the Prophets."

When checked against the Bible, however, these points of comparison prove to be pure fiction.

1. Like Muhammad, Allah sent Jesus as an apostle with a revelation? The Bible affirms that Jesus held legitimate prophethood and spoke for God, John 12:47-50; Hebrews 1:1. But He was so much more than an apostle, Surah 5:75. When one reads about apostles in the New Testament it usually recounts a select group of men, handpicked by Jesus, that met divine qualifications, Matthew 10:1-4; Acts 1:15-26; 1 Corinthians 4:9. These Apostles were witnesses of Jesus Christ – especially of His resurrection, Acts 1:21-22; 2:32; 3:15. They were granted special authority to proclaim the gospel of Jesus Christ, Matthew 28:18-20; Mark 16:15-16; 1 Corinthians 14:37; 2 Peter 3:2; Jude 17. Generally, "apostle" is used to speak of an office directly related to the resurrection and Lordship of Jesus Christ. However, in Hebrews 3:1, the Holy Spirit applies two titles to Jesus Christ Himself, "Apostle" and "High Priest." As Horton and Hurlburt comment:

> Jesus was an apostle (or "Sent One"). He was sent with the Gospel (Good News). God sent prophets and angels to bear His messages to men. He sent Moses, the mighty man of God. But now we are looking at the Apostle from heaven's court itself. He came to bring the most wonderful message ever intended for mortal ears: "God so loved the world!" [2]

Jesus is the "Sent One" from Heaven while Muhammad is not, Hebrews 1:1-2; 3:1. Jesus is the High Priest of the people of God while Muhammad is not, Hebrews 3:1; 4:14-16. Jesus is not a mere apostle like Muhammad claimed to be. He is the Christ!

2. Like Muhammad, Jesus was inspired with a new revelation that confirmed previous revelations? Jesus did not have to correct or revise polluted scriptures, as Muslims say Muhammad had to. The God of the Bible has the power to maintain the integrity of His written word. Jesus said that Scripture cannot be broken, John 10:35. It was not the work of Jesus to reiterate what God had written; rather, He came to fulfill it, Matthew 5:17-18; 26:54, 56. This He did ultimately by His death and resurrection, taking the Old Law out of the way and seating Himself at the right hand of God, John 19:28-30; Colossians 2:11-17; Acts 2:22-36. Jesus did not foretell the arrival of Muhammad (Surah 61:6), because the consummation of God's eternal purposes was in Christ and no other, Ephesians 3:11.

3. Like Muhammad, Jesus was an exalted prophet, receiving special notice and treatment? In the Bible, prophets were not honored and loved during their lifetime because of their work. They were often persecuted, despised, and killed by their brethren only to be falsely honored generations later, Matthew 23:29-35. The fickle masses of ancient Israel treated Jesus after this fashion. One moment they sought to crown Him king, and the next they demanded that He be crucified, John 6:14-15; 19:12-16. How exactly did Jesus receive special notice or treatment? He did not have a home, Matthew 8:20. He did not have a wife, let alone a harem. He did not have earthly riches, Matthew 17:24-27. His family discouraged His work, John 7:3-5. He was rejected by His hometown and eventually by His nation, Luke 4:16, 28-30; 23:20-25. It is difficult indeed to find the Savior's special treatment in the Bible.

4. Like Muhammad, Jesus asked for help to prevail over his enemies? Biblically, Jesus did not turn to men to find aid or relief. He never entrusted Himself to men, John 2:24-25. Should He need assistance, He made it clear that such would come from God, Matthew 26:53. Jesus taught that His kingdom was not of this world, and physical violence to overcome His enemies was condemned, Matthew 26:50-54; Luke 22:49-51; John 18:36. By surrendering and suffering at the hands of His enemies, Jesus overcame the world and remains highly exalted, 1 Peter 2:21-25; John 16:33; 1 John 5:4-5; Philippians 2:5-11.

5. Like Muhammad, Jesus cursed disbelievers? Actually, the Bible teaches that Jesus Christ *became a curse to save* sinners, Galatians 3:13-14. He cursed no one for rejecting Him throughout His incarnation and earthly ministry, John 3:17; 12:47-50. In the moments of greatest persecution and suffering, Jesus remained silent, 1 Peter 2:21-25. When He did cry out from the cross, it was to ask forgiveness upon the transgressors, not revenge, Luke 23:34. The Gospels exist to bring disbelievers to belief (John 20:30-31; Romans 10:17), not to curse them.

Revising Jesus' Claim of Deity

In addition to creating tales and quotes about Jesus, the Qur'an also attempts to erase teachings and events that really happened. Thus, the claims of Jesus are revised. The Qur'an speaks of a Jesus entirely foreign to the Bible.

In the Bible, Jesus claimed to be the Lord – He claimed to be deity. Read the following passages and note that:
- He accepted the title "Christ, Son of God," Matthew 16:13-16; John 11:27.
- He referred to Himself as the "only begotten Son of God," John 3:16-18.
- He is the exclusive way to God, John 14:6; 1 Timothy 2:5-6.
- He claimed to be sinless, something beyond a mere man's capability, John 8:46 compare Romans 3:23.
- He forgave sin, something only God can do, Luke 5:20-21; Mark 2:5-12.
- He is Yahweh, the Great "I Am," John 8:24, 28, 58.
- He is One with God, John 10:30-33.
- He taught authoritatively, Matthew 7:29; John 12:49-50.
- He was killed for this claim, Luke 22:66-71.

Mankind can certainly reject Jesus Christ. Every individual was created with free will. The claim of Christ to be Lord is a crisis point, though. Either an individual accepts it or rejects it. One cannot ignore the words of Jesus, cannot read the Bible and honestly contend He never claimed to be deity. Yet in the Qur'an, that is exactly what one finds: Jesus pleading with Allah that He never said He was deity.

"They are surely infidels who say: 'God is the Christ, son of Mary.' But the Christ had only said: 'O children of Israel, worship God, who is my Lord and your Lord,'" Surah 5:72.

"(Jesus only said:) 'Surely God is my Lord and your Lord, so worship Him. This is the straight path,'" Surah 19:36.

"And when God will ask: 'O Jesus, son of Mary, did you say to mankind: 'Worship me and my mother as two deities apart from God?' (Jesus) will answer: 'Halleluja. Could I say what I knew I had no right (to say)? Had I said it You would surely have known, for You know what is in my heart though I know not what you have. You alone have the secrets unknown. I said nought to them but what You commanded me: Worship God, my Lord and your Lord,'" Surah 5:116-117.

Indeed, Jesus never commanded worshipping Mary. Obviously Surah 5:116 is lashing out at Catholic practices of nearly deifying the virgin mother. However, Jesus accepted those who worshipped Him, according to the Bible, because He was God, Matthew 14:33; Mark 5:6; John 9:38. The Qur'an also changed this fact: Jesus never accepted worship according to it, Surah 5:116-117.

Surah 5:116-117 also introduces a fundamental misunderstanding that many Muslims hold of Christianity pertaining to God. They believe that Christians teach the Godhead is made up of God the Father, Mary, and Jesus Christ. This is not a Biblical doctrine of Godhead, and will be addressed in lesson nine.

Contention over the Virgin Birth – Son of Mary or Son of God?
Muslims believe that Mary was a virgin when Jesus was born. In fact, the Qur'an does not mention Mary's husband Joseph at all. Muslims do not believe that Jesus is the Son of God, or that deity was clothed with flesh in Mary's womb by the power of the Holy Spirit, Luke 1:35; Matthew 1:18. Muslims are quite disturbed by the confession "Jesus is the Son of God," Matthew 16:16; Acts 8:37. To them it means God the Father had relations with a woman and conceived a son. This is quite appalling to Christians as well, and it is certainly not what the New Testament teaches about Mary's miraculous conception, Matthew 1:18-25; Luke 1:26-38.

The Qur'an emphasizes that Jesus is the son of Mary. It gives Him this title twenty-three times in order to stress His humanity and mortality.[3] Jesus is called "son of Mary" once in the Bible, Mark 6:3. This is not a title given by God, but by disbelieving Jews in a derogatory fashion. It is curious how a dishonorable title for

Jesus in the New Testament becomes Allah's title of choice in the Qur'an.

Muhammad boldly denies that Jesus Christ was the Son of God. He reasoned that if Allah had a son, he would be the first to worship him.

"Say: 'If Ar-Rahman had a son I would have been the first of worshippers.' All too glorious is He, Lord of the heavens and the earth, the Lord of all power, for what they ascribe to Him!" Surah 43:81-82

Muhammad mentions the virgin birth of Jesus multiple times, Surah 3:42-51; 19:16-37. While some aspects of Qur'anic accounts echo Biblical truth, there are fundamental differences. The Qur'an maintains Jesus was *created* in the womb of Mary. Jesus is a creature, not the uncreated, eternal God. Jesus is not Emmanuel: God with us. Allah made Jesus just like he made Adam. He spoke him into existence.

"It does not behoove God to have a son. To immaculate is He! When He decrees a thing He has only to say: 'Be,' and it is," Surah 19:35.

"She said: 'How can I have a son, O Lord, when no man has touched me?' He said: 'That is how God creates what He wills. When He decrees a thing, He says 'Be', and it is,'" Surah 3:47.

"For God the likeness of Jesus is as that of Adam whom He fashioned out of dust and said 'Be' and he was," Surah 3:59.

To Muhammad, Jesus was a special prophet, miraculously born of a virgin. Nevertheless He was created, not the Creator. When Muslims affirm the virgin birth of Jesus, they in no way accept that He is the Son of God. They emphasize instead that Jesus is the son of Mary. Allah has no son!

"And say: 'All praise be to God who has neither begotten a son nor has a partner in His kingdom; nor has He need of any one to protect Him from ignominy. So extol Him by extolling His majesty'" Surah 17:111.

"Say: 'He is God the one the most unique, God the immanently indispensable. He has begotten no one, and is begotten of none. There is no one comparable to Him'" Surah 112:1-4.

Islam's Jesus is just an apostle, just the son of Mary. He is not the Son of God, not a king, not worthy of worship, though the Qur'an does speak highly of Him. According to Muhammad, Jesus was not and is not deity. But the Bible affirms the deity of Jesus, John 1:1-3; 8:23-24; Philippians 2:5-9; Revelation 5:11-13.

Signs and Miracles but no Resurrection
Right from the cradle, Islam's Jesus is performing signs and miracles. While the Qur'an offers no signs or miracles that Muhammad worked to corroborate that his

revelations were from God, it says Jesus did amazing things.

"When the angels said: 'O Mary, God gives you news of a thing from Him, for rejoicing, (news of one) whose name will be Messiah, Jesus, son of Mary, illustrious in this world and the next, and one among the honoured, Who will speak to the people when in the cradle and when in the prime of life, and will be among the upright and doers of good [...] He will teach him the Law and the judgment, and the Torah and the Gospel, And he will be Apostle to the children of Israel, (saying:) 'I have come to you with a prodigy from your Lord that I will fashion the state of destiny out of mire for you, and breathe (a new spirit) into it, and (you) will rise by the will of God. I will heal the blind and the leper, and infuse life into the dead, by the leave of God. I will tell you what you devour and what you hoard in your homes. In this will be a portent for you if you believe,'" Surah 5:45-46, 48-49.

"And when God will say: 'O Jesus, son of Mary, remember the favours I bestowed on you and your mother and reinforced you with divine grace, that you spoke to men when in the cradle, and when in the prime of life; when I taught you the law and the judgment and the Torah and the Gospel; when you formed the state of your people's destiny out of mire and you breathed (a new spirit) into it, and they rose by My leave; when you healed the blind by My leave and the leper; when you put life into the dead by My will; and when I held back the children of Israel from you when you brought to them My signs, and the disbelievers among them said: 'Surely these are nothing but pure magic,'" Surah 5:110.

According to the verses quoted above, Allah foretold Jesus' miracle ministry before He was born and then recounted it to Him at a later time. Jesus healed the blind and leprous, even raised the dead, all by Allah's leave. Jesus was the special apostle sent to change Israel's state, but most of the Jews rejected Him. They accused Him of working magic instead of miracles. The New Testament accounts give great detail to the miracles Jesus performed. While He did cleanse lepers and give sight to the blind, He did so much more.

In Islam, Jesus' few disciples asked Him for a sign to assure them that He was who He claimed to be. The Qur'an records Jesus' final and greatest sign. By this miracle the Jews could never again question that He was Allah's apostle. According to the Qur'an, raising the dead and healing lepers was not enough to convince the followers. In Surah 5, we find the final proof of Jesus:

"When the disciples said: 'O Jesus, son of Mary, could your Lord send down for us a table laid with food?' he said: 'Fear God, if indeed you believe.' They said: 'We should like to eat of it to reassure our hearts and to know that it's the truth you have told us, and that we should be witness to it.' Said Jesus, son of Mary, 'O God, our Lord, send down a table well laid with food from the skies

so that this day may be a day of feast for the earlier among us and the later, and a token from You. Give us our (daily) bread, for You are the best of all givers of food.' And said God: 'I shall send it down to you; but if any of you disbelieve after this, I shall inflict such punishment on him as I never shall inflict on any other creature,'" Surah 5:112-115.

A feast! His disciples were witnesses of a feast! The sign of all signs is a feast sent down from Allah? Are Christians to surmise that this is somehow related to the Biblical teaching on the Lord's Supper? 1 Corinthians 11:23-29. Is this a play on Christ's feeding 5,000 men with the fishes and loaves? Matthew 14:15-21. Or is this an echo of Peter's vision teaching that Gentiles may receive the Gospel? Acts 10:9-16. It would be nice to know what that meal consisted of. Consider, after eating, those that yet doubt will receive a hellish punishment unlike any other creature. That is some meal.

In fact, the Bible does teach a consummating miracle – the greatest evidence of the Lordship of Christ: His resurrection. When Jesus laid down His life and took it up again, it was the watershed action of all human history. Everything before looked toward the cross and everything afterward harkens back to the empty tomb!

Islam denies the crucifixion of Jesus Christ ever happened. His death is completely omitted. Obviously then, Islam also denies the resurrection. If Jesus never died, how could He rise again? Islam thus guts Christianity of its core: No Lord Jesus – No Cross – No Resurrection, 1 Corinthians 15:1-22.

"And because they denied and spoke dreadful calumnies of Mary; And for saying, 'We killed the Christ, Jesus, son of Mary, who was an apostle of God;' but they neither killed nor crucified him, though it so appeared to them. Those who disagree in the matter are only lost in doubt. They have no knowledge about it other than conjecture, for surely they did not kill him, But God raised him up (in position) and closer to Himself; and God is all-mighty and all-wise," Surah 4:156-158.

While the Jews tried to crucify Jesus, in the Qur'an they could not. Someone else was crucified, and Muslims disagree about whom that was. Perhaps it was Judas, who was made to appear like Jesus, or even Simon of Cyrene may have been mistakenly crucified.[4] But Jesus Himself was taken away to Allah in some Elijah/Enoch type fashion (2 Kings 2:1-14; Hebrews 11:5) to await the end of time.

"When God said: 'O Jesus, I will take you to Myself and exalt you, and rid you of the infidels, and hold those who follow you above those who disbelieve till the Day of Resurrection. You have then to come back to Me when I will judge between you in what you were at variance,'" Surah 3:55.

Stumbling Block: Confess Jesus or Deny Him?
This lesson began by recognizing that Jesus Christ is the stumbling block

between Islam and Christianity. How can He not be? The Bible and the Qur'an reveal two entirely different beings alike only in name. One account is true and one is false. Every person in the world must decide what to do with Jesus, as the consequences of handling Him wrongly are serious according to both religions.

Obviously [...] Muslims deny that Jesus Christ was God incarnate. Any Muslim who believes that Jesus Christ is God has committed "the one unforgivable sin" called *shirk* – a sin that will send him to hell forever. The Koran clearly teaches that Jesus was only a man: "The Messiah, Jesus son of Mary, was only the Messenger of God [...]" Surah 43:59 asserts: "Jesus was no more than a mortal whom [Allah] favored and made an example to the Israelites."[5]

Shirk is the sin of association. Like Christianity, Islam is a monotheistic religion, asserting there is only one true God. "*Tawhid* is the Muslim doctrine of the singularity of Allah; *shirk* is its opposite, the greatest of all sins and refers to assigning partners or companions to Allah."[6] To believe in the Biblical doctrine of Godhead then is *shirk*, Surah 5:73-74. To confess Jesus Christ that He is the "Son of God" is *shirk*, Surah 5:72. That which is necessary for salvation in Christianity unequivocally damns a soul to hell in Islam.

"And say: 'All praise be to God who has neither begotten a son nor has a partner in His kingdom; nor has He need of any one to protect Him from ignominy. So extol Him by extolling His majesty,'" Surah 17:111.

"They are surely infidels who say: 'God is the Christ, son of Mary.' But the Christ had only said: 'O children of Israel, worship God, who is my Lord and your Lord.' Whosoever associates a compeer with God, will have Paradise denied to him by God, and his abode shall be Hell; and the sinners will have none to help them," Surah 5:72.

"The Christians say: 'Christ is the Son of God.' That is what they say with their tongues following assertions made by unbelievers before them. May they be damned by God: How perverse are they!" Surah 9:30.

There is no middle ground here. The New Testament teaches that if one denies Jesus Christ, or refuses to believe He is the "Son of God," he stands eternally condemned.

"Therefore whoever confesses Me before men, him I will also confess before My Father who is in heaven. But whoever denies Me before men, him I will also deny before My Father who is in heaven," Matthew 10:32-33.

"For God so loved the world that He gave His only begotten Son, that whoever believes in Him should not perish but have everlasting life... He who believes in Him is not condemned; but he who does not believe is condemned already, because he has

not believed in the name of the only begotten Son of God," John 3:16, 18.

"He who believes and is baptized will be saved; but he who does not believe will be condemned," Mark 16:16.

Jesus is the pivotal figure, the stumbling block that causes any notion that Islam and Christianity are sister faiths to falter. Christians cannot recant the truth that He is Lord, and Muslims dare not confess Him as such. His position makes Him impossible to marginalize. Confess Him or reject Him, all mankind must come to a decision about Jesus Christ.

Lesson 8 Questions

1. In what sense might Jesus be viewed as common ground between Islam and Christianity?

2. When a Muslim says, "I believe in Jesus" does that mean the same thing as a Christian confessing "I believe in Jesus"? Why or why not?

3. Define Messiah. What three offices is the Messiah anointed to hold?

4. List at least five ways the Qur'an draws a favorable comparison between Muhammad and Jesus. When the Bible is consulted, do any of these comparisons stand? Explain your answer.

5. What might Muhammad have gained in the seventh century if Muslims and other Arabians viewed him and Jesus in a similar light?

6. Give some instances where the Qur'an and the New Testament differ about the claims of Jesus.

7. How does the Bible version of the virgin birth compare and contrast with the Qur'an's version?

8. The Qur'an mentions some miracles Jesus did that the New Testament confirms. Name them and where such is mentioned in the New Testament.

9. List other miracles Jesus did from the New Testament text.

10. What was Jesus' greatest sign in the Qur'an?

11. What was Jesus' greatest sign in the Bible?

12. How do the Bible and Qur'an differ concerning Jesus' crucifixion?

13. Who do Muslims think was crucified between two thieves?

14. Explain the Islamic doctrine of *shirk*.

15. How is Jesus ultimately a stumbling block dividing Islam and Christianity?

Endnotes

[1] from Nelson's Illustrated Bible Dictionary, Copyright (c)1986, Thomas Nelson Publishers.

[2] Horton, T. C. and Charles E. Hurlburt. Names of Christ. Chicago, IL: Moody Press, 1994. p. 138.

[3] Caner, Ergun Mehmet and Emir Fethi Caner. Unveiling Islam: An Insider's Look at Muslim Life and Beliefs. Grand Rapids, MI: Kregel Publications, 2002. p. 219.

[4] Caner and Caner, p. 220.

[5] Ankerberg, John and John Weldon. The Facts on Islam. Eugene, OR: Harvest House Publishers, 1998. p. 20-21.

[6] Ankerberg and Weldon, p. 61.

Lesson 9
The Lord Our God Is One

"Jesus answered him, 'The first of all the commandments is: 'Hear, O Israel, the Lord our God, the Lord is one,'" Mark 12:29.

There Is A God, He Is Alive

There is a popular misconception held today by many Americans, some of them Christians: Allah of the Qur'an is the same entity as Jehovah God of the Bible, just known by another name. Many people have simply assumed such is the case, and are generally accepting of the mindset that all religions serve the same *higher power* (whatever the name) in their own way. Robert Morey warns against such lethargic thinking toward religion:

> "In the field of comparative religions, it is understood that each of the major religions of mankind has its own peculiar concept of deity. In other words, all religions do not worship the same God, only under different names. The sloppy thinking that would ignore the essential differences which divide world religions is an insult to the uniqueness of world religions."[1]

In reading certain passages of the Qur'an, it is evident that Islam claims to serve the God revealed in the Bible.

"Say: 'We believe in God and what has been sent down to us, and what had been revealed to Abraham and Ishmael and Isaac and Jacob and their progeny, and that which was given to Moses and Christ, and to all other prophets by the Lord. We make no distinction among them, and we submit to Him,'" Surah 2:136.

"Do not argue with the people of the book unless in a fair way, apart from those who act wrongly, and say to them: 'We believe what has been sent down to you. Our God and your God is one, and to Him we submit,'" Surah 29:46.

Is this so? Are people to understand that the Islamic god and Christian God are indeed one? Such a conclusion reduces differences in Islam and Christianity largely to a question of semantics. Ultimately, if it is the same God that Christians and Muslims serve, then it should be the same message that Christians and Muslims preach! It is necessary to step beyond Western culture's comfort zone of religious relativism and recognize that the claims of these two religions are exclusive and opposed to one another. This point is most drastically made studying Jehovah God and Allah from the

Bible and the Qur'an.

Monotheism

Christianity and Islam are both theistic religions. They adhere to a real and active God. It is their understanding of this being and His will which significantly shapes their beliefs and defines their relationship to the world around them.

> Theism is the worldview that holds to the belief that the world is more than just the physical universe (atheism). At the same time, theists do not accept the idea that God is the world (pantheism). They believe in the existence of God and see His existence as the essential component of the theistic worldview. Theists are convinced that the universe had a supernatural First Cause who is infinitely powerful and intelligent. An infinite God is both beyond and manifests Himself in the universe. This God is a personal God, separate from the world, who created the universe and sustains it. Theists believe that God can act within the universe in a supernatural way. The traditional religions of Judaism, Islam, and Christianity represent theism.[2]

The theistic beliefs of Islam and Christianity set them apart from Eastern religions, New Age religions, and all manner of atheism so prevalent in the present age.

In the ancient world, Christianity and Islam set themselves apart from the popular competing belief systems by being monotheistic. They grew to prominence (and perhaps dominance) in polytheistic cultures. Their message of *one* true God was radical to people who sacrificed to a pantheon of crafted and carved deities believed to control carnal matters such as weather, the elements, crops, or fertility. Indeed, the message of monotheism stirred up strong resistance and even persecution from some leaders among polytheistic religions. The ministry of Paul exemplifies the opposition to monotheism in the spread of Christianity throughout the Greco-Roman world, Acts 17:16-34; 19:21-41. Likewise Muhammad had to leave Mecca because he condemned the idolatry of the Ka'bah, Surah 2:163. Arabia had its own mythology of gods including those named Allah, Al-Uzza, Al-Lat, and Manat.[3]

The Bible and the Qur'an proclaim monotheism: one true God.

"Jesus answered him, 'The first of all the commandments is: 'Hear, O Israel, the Lord our God, the Lord is one,'" Mark 12:29.

"You believe that there is one God. You do well. Even the demons believe -- and tremble!" James 2:19.

"Therefore, my beloved, flee from idolatry," 1 Corinthians 10:14.[4]

"Say: 'He is God the One the most unique, God the immanently indispensable. He has begotten no one, and is begotten of none. There is no one comparable to Him,'" Surah 112:1-4.

Faithful Christians and Muslims will always affirm monotheism and take their stand upon it. However, though they may agree there is *one* God, there is much disagreement as to who that God is.

The Names of God

Islam has a clear agenda in blurring the names of deity. The Qur'an teaches that Jews, Christians, and Muslims all serve the same God. The religion has much to gain from saying that semantics is largely responsible for differences. Muhammad's teaching was that his message was the same pure message of submission that Allah had revealed to Jews and Christians. "The people of the book" polluted that message (creating Judaism and Christianity), and Muhammad set it straight. He restored the true religion (Islam) given by the true God (Allah). Consider this study note found in Ahmed Ali's translation of the Qur'an:

> Allah is the name of the same Supreme Being who is called in English God and Khuda in Persian. He is the same God the Jews and Christians worship. "Our God and your God is one," is said in the Qur'an to the people of the book in 29:46. "Whatever name you call Him by, (Allah or Ar-Rahman), all His names are beautiful," Surah 17:110.[5]

According to Islamic tradition, there are ninety-nine names for their god.[6] Allah is the first and best name, because it is the name above all other names and cites the essence of being. All of Allah's names are beautiful, and tend to reveal an attribute which helps define him, Surah 59:22-24. In reality, no formal list of these ninety-nine names is given in the Qur'an, though different lists do exist and have been compiled from the Qur'an and Hadith over the centuries. The 1880 *Journal of the Royal Asiatic Society* researched and published a list of 552 different names for Allah.[7] It seems Muslims have much more freedom in naming their Higher Power than Christians do.

"Nor is there salvation in any other, for there is no other name under heaven given among men by which we must be saved," Acts 4:12.

Accepting that Allah is a fine "nickname" for Jehovah (or vice versa) does not change the fact that Christians and Muslims do not pray to the same God. Choosing the name of Allah either does disservice to both religions (ignoring the unique features of each Being), or it asserts the superiority of Islam (the Qur'an teaches that Allah is, in fact, the actual Jehovah who revealed the Bible). Roberts warns that Christians dare not concede that "Allah" is an accurate and acceptable name for their God:

> The god of Islam, Allah, simply is not the same as Jehovah. To say otherwise is to make the same mistake of Hosea's day, when Israel in utter

confusion and ignorance addressed the Lord as Baal, Hosea 2:16ff. Yes, Baal could mean "Lord" but calling Jehovah "Baal" was wrong. Similarly, calling Jehovah "Allah" is wrong today. Allah is the god of Islam, a single being that has no triune nature, has no desire for relationship with his creatures, and is absolutely unknowable. Allah may share some similarities with Jehovah, but certainly is not Jehovah and Christians err greatly when they try to equate these two.[8]

Morey focused on the significance of differences between Allah and the Christian's God when he wrote:

Islam claims that Allah is the same God who was revealed in the Bible. This logically implies in the positive sense that the concept of God set forth in the QUR'AN will correspond in all points to the concept of God found in the Bible. This also implies in the negative sense that if the Bible and the QUR'AN have differing views of God, then Islam's claim is false.[9]

As we will see, Jehovah and Allah differ in more than their names. They are not the same God. Consequently, as Islam and Christianity are both monotheistic religions – meaning that they believe there is only one true God – then by definition at least one of these gods is false, created by men and not the eternal Creator.

Jehovah and Allah: Different Nature

Allah's nature is Unitarian. According to *Webster's Collegiate Dictionary*, "Unitarian" is the belief that the deity exists in only one person. Islam teaches that there is no Godhead; there is only one God – Allah – and he is singular in nature. Allah is the sole being that possesses all qualities of divinity and is the essence of deity.

"So believe in God and His apostles, and do not call Him 'Trinity.' Abstain from this for your good; for God is only one God, and far from His glory is it to beget a son. All that is in the heavens and the earth belongs to Him; and sufficient is God for all help," Surah 4:171b.

"They consider their rabbis and monks and the Christ, son of Mary, to be gods apart from God, even though they had been enjoined to worship only one God, for there is no god but He. Too holy is He for what they ascribe to Him!" Surah 9:31.

"And say: 'All praise be to God who has neither begotten a son nor has a partner in His kingdom; nor has He need of any one to protect Him from ignominy. So extol Him by extolling His majesty,'" Surah 17:111.

The Islamic doctrine of *shirk* guards this Unitarian concept of monotheism. *Shirk* – meaning "association" – is the taking of some aspect of the created world and giving it the worship and service that Allah deserves. Simply put, this association constitutes idolatry.[10] According to the Qur'an, *shirk* is the unforgivable sin.

"God does not forgive that compeers be ascribed to Him, though He may forgive aught else if He please. And he who ascribes compeers to God is guilty of the greatest sin," Surah 4:48.

"Whosoever associates a compeer with God, will have Paradise denied to him by God, and his abode shall be Hell; and the sinners will have none to help them. Disbelievers are they surely who say: 'God is the third of the trinity;' but there is no God other than God the one," Surah 5:72-73.

The Bible condemns idolatry throughout the testaments, Exodus 20:4-5; 1 John 5:21. But *shirk* has implications for Christians beyond graven images. As was seen in the last lesson, Muslims believe that Jesus was created. They believe that Allah created Jesus, just as he created Adam, Surah 3:47, 59. This means that Jesus is part of creation, and if people worship Him as God or confess Him as the Son of God, they have committed *shirk*. In Muhammad's eyes, the "good confession" (Matthew 16:16; Acts 8:35-39; Romans 10:9-10) was actually *shirk* and idolatry damning the soul to Hell-fire.

"The Christians say: 'Christ is the son of God.' That is what they say with their tongues following assertions made by unbelievers before them. May they be damned by God: How perverse are they!" Surah 9:30.

Both the Biblical doctrines of Godhead and the deity of Christ are *shirk*. As such, Christians, or "the people of the book," get special attention from Allah's prophet.

"Tell them: 'O people of the book let us come to an agreement on that which is common between us, that we worship no one but God, and make none His compeer, and that none of us take any others for lord apart from God.' If they turn away you tell them: 'Bear witness that we submit to Him,'" Surah 3:64.

Clearly, Allah's nature is Unitarian, and the Qur'an pronounces serious consequences for those who associate any with him – in other words, those who commit *shirk*! The Bible reveals a God with a very different nature. While the Bible consistently proclaims there is only one God, the God of the Bible has a triune nature. The Bible teaches that there is a Godhead, Romans 1:20; Acts 17:29; Colossians 2:9.[11]

The word "Godhead" is from the Greek word "Theios."[12] *Thayer's Greek Lexicon* defines "Theios" as "deity, the state of being God: Godhead." Godhead means deity, divine nature. It is the essence of God with the fullness of divine attributes. As Christians speak of the number of persons in the Godhead or divine nature, they speak of the number possessing divinity and whose essence is deity.

The divine nature or Godhead consists of three distinct persons, each possessing all the attributes of divinity and deity. This means that the Father, Son, and Holy Spirit are fully God.

- The Father is called God, 1 Corinthians 1:3; 8:6; 2 John 3: Jude 1.
- Jesus Christ is called God, John 1:1-3, 14; 2 Peter 1:1; Titus 2:13.
- The Holy Spirit is called God, Acts 5:1-4.

Let it be understood that Christians do not believe Mary is God or is ever called God. She is not associated with the Godhead or a part of the triune nature of God. Christians do not believe that God the Father had relations with Mary to conceive and bear Jesus. However, this is what many Muslims believe Christians mean when they speak of the triune nature of God or deity of Jesus. They believe this because Muhammad supplied this corrupt view of the Godhead.

"And when God will ask: 'O Jesus, son of Mary, did you say to mankind: 'Worship me and my mother as two deities apart from God?' (Jesus) will answer: 'Hallelujah. Could I say what I knew I had no right (to say)?'" Surah 5:116.

"O people of the book, do not be fanatical in your faith, and say nothing but the truth about God. The Messiah who is Jesus, son of Mary, was only an apostle of God, and a command of His which He sent to Mary, as a mercy from Him. So believe in God and His apostles, and do not call Him 'Trinity.' Abstain from this for your good; for God is only one God, and far from His glory is it to beget a son. All that is in the heavens and the earth belongs to Him; and sufficient is God for all help," Surah 4:171.

According to the Bible, Mary was not divine. Furthermore, she did not conceive by any natural processes. She was a virgin, Isaiah 7:14; Luke 1:34; Matthew 1:25. God the Son was placed in her womb miraculously by God the Holy Spirit, Matthew 1:18; Luke 1:35. God the Son was never created; rather, He was incarnated, the Immanuel, to fulfill God the Father's purposes, Isaiah 7:14; Matthew 1:23; John 1:14, 18.

The Father, the Son, and the Holy Spirit are all three God, but they are separate and distinct from one another.

- God the Son is not God the Father. Jesus Christ distinctly came to do the Father's will, John 8:28-29; 12:48-49; 14:28; Philippians 2:5-11.
- God the Son is not God the Holy Spirit. The Holy Spirit distinctly came to the apostles only after the resurrection and ascension of Jesus Christ, John 16:5-15; Acts 1:4-8; 2.
- God the Father is not God the Holy Spirit. The Holy Spirit distinctly brought the Father's will from His mind and inspired the apostles, prophets, and Biblical writers, John 16:13-15; 1 Corinthians 2:9-13; 2 Timothy 3:16-17; 2 Peter 1:20-21.
- God the Father, God the Son, and God the Holy Spirit each had a distinct form, role, and place at the baptism of Jesus, Matthew 3:16-17.

This is the Bible's stand on Jehovah God's nature and being. He is One, and He is Godhead. While Godhead may be a challenging concept to grasp, it is no less Biblical, Matthew 28:20; 2 Corinthians 13:14. Human beings are not in the position to criticize or place limitations on God's nature or revelation of His nature. Humans and their understanding are finite, while God is infinite, Isaiah 55:8-9.

Saal suggests that illustrations may be helpful in understanding the concept of Godhead and sharing it with others:

> Diversity in the unity of the Creator is reflected in what He made and in human thought. To be sure, all illustrations are inadequate, but they do help us think. Humans think in picture language, and despite Muslim sensitivities, it is wise to follow the example of our Lord and use good pictures, appropriate to our listener, rather than to do without. Here are a few concrete suggestions:
> - The one chemical substance of H_2O is always present in its three different forms – solid, liquid, and vapor.
> - We experience a flame in its shape, its light, and its heat. (It is possible to see a certain analogy: the form suggests the supreme authority of the Father, the light the revealing role of the Son, the heat the invisible influence of the Spirit. The sun can also be used in this way.) […]
> - To understand the world around us, we think in three dimensions. Space is one, but we know it in three dimensions.[13]

This is a fundamental difference between Allah and Jehovah. Allah knows no Holy Spirit, nor would he claim Jesus or any other as son. But the God of the Bible said the Holy Spirit knows His thoughts (1 Corinthians 2:11), and said of Jesus, "This is My beloved Son, in whom I am well pleased," Matthew 3:17. Clearly, Jehovah God and Allah have different natures and cannot be the same being!

Jehovah and Allah: Different Attributes

For the Islamic claim to be true that the God of the Bible and Allah of the Qur'an are one and the same, then both Jehovah and Allah must have the same nature and attributes. They do not possess the same nature. But what about the same attributes? Let's look at four examples which sustain that Jehovah's attributes and Allah's attributes are different, exclusive, and even antagonistic.

1. The God who Loves His Enemies OR The God who Hates His Enemies?

The Bible says that Jehovah God is love, 1 John 4:8. He does not wait for love to be shown to Him and then reciprocates; rather, God initiates love, 1 John 4:10,19. One of the greatest truths of the Bible is that God loved humanity despite their grievous sins against Him. When humanity was helpless and unlovable in every respect, God's love shown forth and acted on humanity's behalf, Romans 5:6-8. Jehovah demonstrated His unconditional love for the world by sacrificing Jesus Christ, John 3:16. The love of Jehovah is not like the love of men. His love is perfect, pure, and the standard that Christians strive for. Jehovah loves even His enemies, and He always has.

"You have heard that it was said, 'You shall love your neighbor and hate your enemy.' But I say to you, love your enemies, bless those who curse you, do good to those who hate you, and pray for those who spitefully use you and persecute you, that you may be sons of your Father in heaven; for He makes His sun rise on the evil and on the good, and sends rain on the just and on the unjust. For if you love those who love you, what reward have you? Do not even the tax collectors do the same? And if you greet your brethren only, what do you do more than others? Do not even the tax collectors do so? Therefore you shall be perfect, just as your Father in heaven is perfect," Matthew 5:43-48.

Allah does not love his enemies, nor does he initiate love or a loving relationship with sinners, Surah 2:98. While Allah reciprocates love for the Muslim who obeys Muhammad, he has only hate for the disbeliever (sinner, infidel, Christian).

"Say: 'If you love God then follow me that God may love you and forgive your faults; for God is forgiving and kind.' Say: 'Obey God and His Messenger;' and if they refuse (then remember) God does not love disbelievers," Surah 3:31-32.

2. The God who is Relational OR The God who is Non-Relational?

The Bible teaches that people can know God and have a relationship with Him through Jesus Christ. In fact, Jehovah offers a family relationship: sinners who are alienated can be forgiven and adopted as sons and daughters, Galatians 3:26-27; 4:4-7. Christians are children of God because of His amazing love and gift of Jesus Christ, 1 John 3:1-3; Romans 6:23. This intimate relationship with God is a unique feature of Biblical Christianity.

"Behold what manner of love the Father has bestowed on us, that we should be called children of God! [...] Beloved, now we are children of God [...]," 1 John 3:1-2.

Allah has no children! Jesus Christ is certainly not his son, and Allah is not interested in having an earthly family. Recall the popular Muslim tradition that Allah has ninety-nine beautiful names. "Father" is not on the list. In fact, it would be unfitting (possibly *shirk*) for a Muslim to address Allah with such a familiar and intimate term. Allah is the distant, unaffiliated Creator of mortals. There is no assurance that he acts lovingly, with the best interest of his followers at heart. Instead he often deals arbitrarily with his creation, as a despot over his subjects.

"Say the Jews and the Christians: 'We are sons of God and beloved of Him.' Say: 'Why does He punish you then for your sins? No: You are only mortals, of His creation.' He can punish whom He please and pardon whom He will, for God's is the kingdom of the heavens and the earth and all that lies between them, and everything will go back to Him," Surah 5:18.

The Qur'an lists many people whom Allah does not love, like sinners, the unjust, and the arrogant, Surahs 2:190; 2:276; 3:57; 4:36. While these are not likeable qualities, Jehovah God nonetheless loves sinners and seeks to redeem them in Christ, Romans 5:8. Jehovah God loves first, while Allah only "loves" those who first love him!

3. The God who is Trustworthy OR The God who is Capricious?

Jehovah says His words will last forever, and His Scripture cannot be broken, Isaiah 55:10-11; Matthew 24:35; John 10:35; 12:48. He does not lie or trick His people (Hebrews 6:18), and He is unchangeable, Malachi 3:6; Hebrews 13:8. Thus, Jehovah can be trusted. While humanity has the prerogative to believe Jehovah or reject Him, they can choose with certainty, because His message is clear, understandable, and unchanging. Jehovah is faithful to His word.

"The entirety of Your word is truth, And every one of Your righteous judgments endures forever," Psalm 119:160.

Allah's word has been changed. If one concedes to Muslims that Allah revealed the Bible, then one must accept that Allah's word has been corrupted by Jews and Christians. Allah could not keep it pure. Furthermore, one must accept Allah's way of abrogation, allowing Him to re-write things he said in the Bible when he revealed the Qur'an through Muhammad. Abrogation also allows the Qur'an to contradict itself. What prevents Allah from changing his mind again and abrogating all of Islam? What safeguards are in place over the purity of the Qur'an? Why would Allah maintain the integrity of the Qur'an from corruptive influences when he would not protect the Bible? Allah changes his word when he fancies it; it is his prerogative according to Islam. It is difficult to put one's trust in such "scripture."

Furthermore, Allah has changed his word in times past to benefit friends! Consider Allah's law for the number of wives that a Muslim man can take: only four wives, Surah 4:3. Yet Muhammad exceeded that number by at least six, and possibly ten. This was with Allah's approval.

"We have made lawful for you, O Prophet, wives to whom you have given their dower, and God-given maids and captives you have married, and the daughters of your father's brothers and daughters of your father's sisters, and daughters of your mother's brothers and sisters, who migrated with you; and a believing woman who offers herself to the Prophet if the Prophet desires to marry her. This is a privilege only for you and not the other believers. We know what We have ordained for them about their wives and maids they possess, so that you may be free of blame, for God is forgiving and kind," Surah 33:50.

When Muhammad went so far as to take another man's wife (the wife of his adopted son, Zaid), Allah not only changed his word to allow Muhammad to exceed four wives, but also endorsed the abominable practice of a father *knowing* his son's wife, compare 1 Corinthians 5:1-2.

"No believing men and women have any choice in a matter after God and His Apostle have decided it. Whoever disobeys God and His Apostle has clearly lost the way and gone astray. When you said to him who had been favored by God and was favored by you: 'Keep your wife to yourself and fear God,' you were hiding something God was about to bring to light, for you had fear of men, though you should fear God more. And when Zaid was through with her, We gave her to you in marriage, so that it may not remain a sin for the faithful (to marry) the wives of their adopted sons when they are through with them. God's command is to be fulfilled. There is no constraint on the Prophet in what God has decreed for him. This has been the way of God with (apostles) who have gone before you, - and God's command is a determined act," Surah 33:36-38.

Allah is absolute and arbitrary! He is capricious and untrustworthy! How can this be the same God as the Jehovah found in the Bible?

It must be difficult for Muslims to serve a god who may change his mind and his word on a whim. Muslims believe that if Allah were consistent it would impugn his sovereignty in some way. How distressing that Allah will be just as capricious when it comes to judgment and the eternal abode of a Muslim's soul.

"To God belongs all that is in the heavens and the earth; and whether you reveal what is in your heart or conceal it, you will have to account for it to God who will pardon whom He please and punish whom He will, for God has the power over all things," Surah 2:284.

4. The God who is Active in History OR The God who is Passive in History?

The eternal God the Son was willing to leave the sanctuary of Heaven to insert Himself into linear time and take an active role in the salvation of the world, Philippians 2:5-8; Hebrews 2:17-18; John 3:16. He traded a throne for a manger, leaving glory for the hostile hill of Calvary.

Jesus was the ultimate manifestation of the God who is active in history, 1 Timothy 3:16. The eternal Word became flesh and dwelt among mankind, John 1:1-3, 14. Jesus was the Immanuel of prophecy, "God with us," Matthew 1:23. Jehovah is the God who takes matters into His own hands when it comes to saving His beloved, and His hands are capable and sufficient. God actively and personally paid the price for the forgiveness of sins.

"[...] He has appeared to put away sin by the sacrifice of Himself. And as it is appointed for men to die once, but after this the judgment, so Christ was offered once to bear the sins of many. To those who eagerly wait for Him He will appear a second time, apart from sin, for salvation," Hebrews 9:26-28.

Allah always "works" from a distance. He is too gloriously transcendent to be thought of in terms of mortality. He "works" through angels, prophets, Muhammad, or the Qur'an. There is always some channel between Allah and the world. He never became the Word incarnate. He never sacrificed for his creation. In fact, the notion that human beings were made in the image of God is completely foreign to Islam, Genesis 1:26-27. The Qur'an never suggests human beings were made in the image of Allah. He is too great!

Clearly, Jehovah God and Allah have different attributes! This cannot be the same God only known by different names.

Jehovah and Allah: Different Supreme Revelation

Jehovah God's supreme revelation was Himself; that is, God in flesh, the person of Jesus Christ, John 1:1-3, 14; 1 Timothy 3:16.

"God, who at various times and in different ways spoke in time past to the fathers by the prophets, has in these last days spoken to us by His Son, whom He has appointed heir of all things, through whom also He made the worlds; who being the brightness of His glory and the express image of His person, and upholding all things by the word of His power, when He had by Himself purged our sins, sat down at the right hand of the Majesty on high," Hebrews 1:1-3.

Jesus Christ was the Immanuel of prophecy, "God with us," Matthew 1:23. As Jesus walked the earth, His unique ministry revealed God. His very being revealed God, because He was the Son of God, God incarnate. As Moser notes:

> What Jesus is, what He taught, what He did, how He felt toward sinners, how He sacrificed Himself for us – in all these things He reveals Himself and the Father. By His life Jesus glorified God, John 17:4. It could not have been otherwise "For in him dwells all the fullness of the Godhead bodily," Colossians 2:9. […] Hence, if we would know what God would say, listen to Jesus; if we would know what the Father would do, watch the Son; if we would know how God feels toward humanity, learn of Christ; in short, if we would know God, know Christ.[14]

Jesus also revealed God by His teaching. As an example, consider some of the parables, Matthew 13; Luke 15. A parable is commonly defined as an earthly story with a heavenly meaning. Jesus' ability to communicate profound spiritual truths in relatable illustrations is unparalleled. What He revealed was the value and values of God's kingdom. He revealed that God is a loving Father, always seeking the "lost sheep" and "lost coin." This was being accomplished, even then, through Jesus Christ, and subsequently by the proclamation of the gospel, Mark 16:15-16; Romans 1:16; 2 Thessalonians 2:14.

Finally, Jesus revealed God by His dealings with men. The Bible says that Jehovah worked through Jesus in unique ways. Studying the interactions of Jesus with others shows more than good works and godliness; Jesus' actions manifest God.

"Then Jesus answered and said to them, 'Most assuredly, I say to you, the Son can do nothing of Himself, but what He sees the Father do; for whatever He does, the Son also does in like manner,'" John 5:19.

"[...] He who has seen Me has seen the Father; so how can you say, 'Show us the Father'? Do you not believe that I am in the Father, and the Father in Me? The words that I speak to you I do not speak on My own authority; but the Father who dwells in Me does the works. Believe Me that I am in the Father and the Father in Me [...]," John 14:9-11.

On the other hand, Allah's supreme revelation is a book, the Qur'an. The extent of his manifestation is allowing people to read about how great he is. Muslims contend that the Qur'an is like Allah, uncreated and perfect in every way.

"This is indeed the glorious Qur'an (Preserved) on the guarded tablet," Surah 85:21-22.

"Those who reject the Reminder when it has come to them (should know) that it is a Book inviolate. Falsehood cannot enter it from any side: It's a revelation from the all-wise and praiseworthy (God)," Surah 41:41-42.

Yet the Qur'an is marred by contradiction, inaccuracy, repetition, and abrogation. Furthermore, it has been corrected in times past for both content and style.[15]

There is nothing in Islam that compares to Jehovah God's manifestation in Jesus Christ, or can contend with His sacrifice for the world. Instead of trying to compete with it, the Qur'an denies that it happened or ever could have happened. Apparently, Allah is far too transcendent and capricious to stoop to such sacrificial love. But this is a huge difference between Jehovah and Allah, and should convince all that they are not the same God.

There Can Only Be One

Jehovah and Allah are not the same God called by different names. Neither Christians nor Muslims should allow such teaching to persist. They differ in nature, attributes, and supreme revelation. All would do well to ponder these words from the Qur'an:

"Say: 'O YOU unbelievers, I do not worship what you worship, nor do you worship who I worship, Nor will I worship what you worship, Nor will you worship who I worship: To you your way, to me my way,'" Surah 109:1-6.

There is a difference between the "who" and "what" that people choose to worship. That is, there is a "who" – a genuine, personal God; and there is a "what" – a god, fashioned by men.

Jehovah or Allah; one is a false god. One conceived the universe in His mind, while the other was conceived in the mind of a man. Who will you believe, love, and serve?

Lesson 9 Questions

1. Why would Muslims say that Islam and Christianity serve the same God?

2. Do you think Islam would flourish or falter in a society where people believed basically all religions serve the same higher power? Why?

3. How do you think Christianity is faring in a society that increasingly accepts that all religions serve the same higher power? Explain.

4. Define Monotheism.

5. How have Christians (and Muslims) suffered in the past for being monotheists?

6. Do you sometimes feel that people in current culture are too ambivalent toward God?

7. How do you strengthen your personal faith in God?

8. Is there anything in a name? Is it important to address God by a scripturally accurate name?

9.Explain the differences between "Triune" and "Unitarian" natures of God.

10. What is the common misunderstanding Muslims have about the Godhead?

11. List and explain the four differences in attributes between Jehovah and Allah.

12. What was Jehovah's supreme revelation?

13. What was Allah's supreme revelation?

14. Make two columns. From your studies thus far, list the similarities between Jehovah and Allah in one column. List the differences between Jehovah and Allah in the second column. Prepare to share and discuss your list.

Endnotes

[1] Morey, Robert. The Islamic Invasion. Las Vegas, NV: Christian Scholars Press, 1992. p.53.

[2] Geisler, Norman and Peter Bocchino. Unshakable Foundations. Minneapolis, MN: Bethany House Publishers, 2001. p. 60.

[3] Investigate the so-called "Satanic Verses" of Surah 53:19-23. Some evidence suggests these verses (at least at one time) attributed three daughters to Allah, which would serve to support the conclusion that Islam is Muhammad's revision of Arabian polytheism, and that his doctrine of Unitarian monotheism developed over a period of time. It also shows that the Qur'an is not beyond corruption and has been corrected.

[4] Monotheism is the consistent doctrine of the Old Testament as well as the New Testament. See also Deuteronomy 6:4, 12-15; 18:9-14; 1 John 5:21; Galatians 5:19-21; 1 Thessalonians 1:8-10.

[5] Ali, Ahmed. AL-QUR'AN: A Contemporary Translation. Princeton, NJ: Princeton University Press, 2001. p. 11.

[6] For lists of Allah's ninety-nine names, see: Geisler, Norman and Abdul Saleeb. Answering Islam. Grand Rapids, MI: Baker, 1993. pp. 21-25. OR Caner, Ergun Mehmet and Emir Fethi Caner. Unveiling Islam: An Insider's Look at Muslim Life and Beliefs. Grand Rapids, MI: Kregel Publications, 2002.pp. 110-117.

[7] Geisler, Norman and Abdul Saleeb. Answering Islam. Grand Rapids, MI: Baker, 1993. p. 21.

[8] Roberts, Mark. "What I Would Say to My Muslim Neighbor." If I Had One Opportunity: Urgent Messages For Today. Ed. Daniel W. Petty. Temple Terrace, FL: Florida College Book Store, 2004. pp. 93-94.

[9] Morey, Robert. The Islamic Invasion. Las Vegas, NV: Christian Scholars Press, 1992. p.57.

[10] Hutchison, John A. Paths of Faith. 4th ed. New York: McGraw-Hill, Inc.,1991 p. 439.

[11] For a clear and concise presentation of Godhead as well as a good study of God the Holy Spirit see Hardin, Michael. The Holy Spirit: His Personality and Work. Bowling Green, KY: Guardian of Truth Foundation, 1996. pp. 6-8.

[12] Recent English translations of the Bible such as the NASB or NIV render "Theios" as "Divine Nature" or "Deity" in Romans 1:20; Acts 17:29; Colossians 2:9.

[13] Saal, William J. Reaching Muslims for Christ. Chicago, IL: Moody Press, 1991. p. 109.

[14] Moser, K.C. Attributes of God. Austin TX: R.B. Sweet Co., Inc., 1963. pp. 14-15.

[15] Review lessons 3 and 4 for specific instances and documentation.

Lesson 10
Who is Your Savior?

"For the grace of God that brings salvation has appeared to all men [...] looking for the blessed hope and glorious appearing of our great God and Savior Jesus Christ," Titus 2:11, 13.

The Consequence of Creation

Both Islam and Christianity promote the concept of linear time. The Bible and the Qur'an teach that time had a starting point, meaning when God acted and created the world, time began, Genesis 1:1; Surah 7:54. Furthermore, time will come to an end, 2 Peter 3:10; Surah 2:62. At the discretion of God, this world will be destroyed, and its inhabitants will stand in judgment before their Creator.

The logical consequence of faith in a Creator is an ultimate judgment. Every architect has the responsibility to evaluate the structure that has been erected under his oversight. Manufacturing companies inspect the quality of their product. Likewise, Christianity and Islam affirm that an intelligent Being has created this world with purpose, and He will determine if that purpose has been accomplished. The Creator will judge humanity. Those souls that are satisfactory in His sight will be rewarded, and those souls that are unacceptable will be condemned. Thus these belief systems are concerned with how the soul shall fair in the hands of its Maker.

In both religions, God is called just, Surah 6:115; Psalm 7:11. He will serve justice – righting all wrongs, punishing the wicked, and rewarding righteousness on the Day of Judgment. It is a common belief between the religions that everyone will face God as Judge:

"Every soul will know the taste of death. You will get your recompense in full on the Day of Resurrection; and he who is spared the Fire and finds his way to Paradise will meet his desire. As for the life of this world, it is nothing but a merchandise of vanity," Surah 3:185.

AND

"Let us hear the conclusion of the whole matter:
Fear God and keep His commandments,
For this is the whole duty of man.
For God will bring every work into judgment,
Including every secret thing,
Whether it is good or whether it is evil," Ecclesiastes 12:13-14.

AND

"And then you will certainly die, Then will be raised up on the Day of Resurrection," Surah 23:15-16.

AND

"But the day of the Lord will come as a thief in the night, in which the heavens will pass away with a great noise, and the elements will melt with fervent heat; both the earth and the works that are in it will be burned up. Therefore, since all these things will be dissolved, what manner of persons ought you to be in holy conduct and godliness," 2 Peter 3:10-11.

Sin

Both the Bible and Qur'an show that the majority of mankind will not fair well at the final judgment. The Qur'an speaks of infidels, idolaters, and transgressors: those who knew Allah's way and received his book, yet did not follow the "straight path." Allah will condemn them.

The Bible also speaks of sin.
- Sin is ultimately and always against God, Psalm 41:4; 51:4.
- Sin is transgression of God's will – rebellion and lawlessness, 1 John 3:4.
- Sin is neglect and omission of God's perfect will, James 4:17.
- Sin is falling short of God's perfect standard, Romans 3:23.
- Sin is of the devil and not of God, 1 John 1:5; 3:6, 8.
- Sin severs fellowship between God and man, Isaiah 59:1-2.
- All accountable people are guilty of sin, Romans 3:23; 7:9.

Clearly the Bible does not take sin lightly. It is severe, ugly, and dangerous. Moser wrote of sin:

"Sin [...] is the manifestation of the presence of Satan as it is proof of the absence of God [...] Sin means enmity against God and agreement with Satan. It is rebellion against God and submission to Satan. Sin is ungodliness and the sinner ungodly [...] Sin is more than simply doing what God says not to do, or failure to do what He commands. It is opposition to God Himself. It is enmity and rebellion. To sin is to offend God personally, because His laws reflect His character. To sin is to join hands with Satan, to be like him, to be of him."[1]

The Bible reveals the most stringent consequences for sin, Romans 6:23; 2 Thessalonians 1:8-9. Eternal separation from God in the torments of Hell is the spiritual death pronounced upon sinners (Matthew 25:41, 46; Mark 9:43-48), and no one speaks more about this fate in the New Testament than Jesus Christ. Jesus said:

"And do not fear those who kill the body but cannot kill the soul. But rather fear Him who is able to destroy both soul and body in hell," Matthew 10:28.

The Bible does not teach that the consequence of sin is, "You need to do a good deed to make up for it." Sin cannot be made up for; it must be paid for, Romans 6:23. Some believers in Christ have erred in times past, teaching that a system of penitence could make up for sin. For instance, it was taught that a number of rote prayers could merit forgiveness of a lie, or that alms could merit forgiveness of theft. The Bible reveals no such system of moral/spiritual weights and measures. What scripture teaches that one sin is worse than another in God's eyes? What scripture teaches that a good work can cancel sin in God's eyes? Even if true restitution could be made to a neighbor one has sinned against on earth, how could one "make it up" to God? Mark 8:36-37. That is who they have ultimately sinned against.

"Against You, You only, have I sinned, And done this evil in Your sight --That You may be found just when You speak, And blameless when You judge," Psalm 51:4.

> "Sin is not simply a passive disregard of God, but an active opposition to Him. God must regard sin as He regards the devil, for sin is of the devil [...] Sin and the sinner cannot be divorced. Sin results in guilt. Just as God's wrath is against sin, so is His wrath upon the sinner. And here is spiritual death – the state of the soul separated from God and joined to Satan."[2]

The Bible states that the cost of sin is death, Romans 6:23. Furthermore, there is nothing man can do of himself to rectify his sin before God. Man cannot merit forgiveness of sin in the eyes of Holy God; he cannot "make it up." It is a truly miserable plight that a sinner finds himself in, and remember all have sinned, Romans 3:23! That means that all are in jeopardy. If mankind is unable to save itself from the consequences of sin, there needs to be a savior. God graciously provided a Savior and means of salvation, Ephesians 2:1-10; Romans 5:6-10; Titus 2:11-14. That is the good news – gospel – of Jesus Christ, Romans 1:16; Mark 16:15-16; Acts 4:12!

How Much Does A Sin Weigh?
Muhammad's "revelation" of the Qur'an brought many revisions of true Scripture, including a tremendous shift concerning sin. In the Qur'an, the state of a sinner is hardly desperate. Muslims do not need a savior. The Qur'an teaches that good works can add up to compensate for transgressions against Allah.

"Remember that good deeds nullify the bad," Surah 11:114.

Recall that Islam is submission. When one converts to Islam, they are converting to a lifestyle of meritorious works. They perform good deeds which hopefully outweigh their bad deeds. "Muslims do not refer to their deliverance as salvation or conversion, but as remembering or returning. Islamic theology is clear that each people group has a messenger, and thereby they know the truth and must return to it."[3]

Islam is devoid of forgiveness based upon any type of sacrifice. As Muhammad revised key Old Testament accounts of Israel, he continually omitted an important recurring element – animal sacrifice. For example, Muhammad repeats his version of the Exodus over and over without ever mentioning the Passover, Exodus 12! In Surah 2:62-71, Muhammad says Allah commanded the Israelites to sacrifice a *yellow* cow at Mount Sinai merely as a test of obedience. Muhammad did not "confirm" the atonement teaching of Old Testament sacrifices. There is no foundation for the sacrifice of Christ to be meaningful in Islam, Hebrews 9:11-10:18. This is, of course, irrelevant as the Qur'an denies that Jesus even died on the cross, Surah 4:156-158.

To Muslims, sacrifices were purely pagan constructs. Allah is spiritual and is not moved by an animal's meat and blood to forgive, Surah 22:37-38. Christians do not practice animal sacrifices today because Jesus Christ was the ultimate sacrifice for the sins of the world, John 1:29; Hebrews 9:11-10:18. However, in Islam, Muslims still practice animal sacrifices. These are largely connected to the special rites a Muslim performs during the *hajj* (pilgrimage to Mecca). The significance of animal sacrifices in Islam is that man holds dominion over the earth and Allah is good to provide food. Muslims teach that the Biblical view of animal sacrifices for atonement (which foreshadowed the sacrifice of Jesus) is evidence that Jews and Christians corrupted the Scriptures with pagan ways.

No substitutionary death is necessary in Islam. Humans transgress against Allah, and humans can make it right by performing good deeds, Surah 39:53-63; 11:114. This is a true religion of works. There is no grace, and there is no savior. It is the Muslim against himself. Will he do more good or more evil in his lifetime? While on the surface that may sound reasonable and comforting, it does great harm to both the creator and the creation.

The system of works is harmful to Allah, as it allows sin against him to go unpunished. To paraphrase Islam's judgment: "Put the deeds of a man on the scale, if there are more good ones than evil ones, then punishment is withheld from that man," Surah 7:7-10. But what of the evil deeds that remain on the other side of the man's scale? Allah must wink at it? How is his justice satisfied? How can Allah allow any wrong to go un-righted, any sin to remain unpunished on the final Day of Reckoning and remain just? In essence, this plan means that Allah will tolerate injustices. Yet this is antagonistic to his nature if he is absolutely just.

The system of works is also harmful to Muslims. There is no revelation telling them how many good works are necessary. The list of good works is long in Islam, as is the list of sins. But nowhere is the Muslim told how much a good work or evil deed weighs. They have no idea how their deeds will stack up on the Last Day. Muslims have to keep doing good all their life, never knowing if it will be enough. There is no hope or assurance about the future to be found in such a system.

Further clouding the already vague arrangement of the scales is the capricious sovereignty of Allah, Surah 3:129. He is not bound to keep his own rules, and he is a respecter of persons.

"To God belongs all that is in the heavens and the earth; and whether you reveal what is in your heart or conceal it, you will have to account for it to God who will pardon whom He please and punish whom He will, for God has the power over all things," Surah 2:284.

Because of Allah's sovereignty, many Muslims believe strongly in predestination and are very fatalistic in their outlook on life.

Muslims believe in *Al-Qadar*, which is divine predestination, but this belief in divine predestination does not mean that human beings do not have freewill. Rather, Muslims believe that God has given human beings freewill. This means that they can choose right or wrong and that they are responsible for their choices.

The belief in divine predestination includes belief in four things: 1) God knows everything. He knows what has happened and what will happen. 2) God has recorded all that has happened and all that will happen. 3) Whatever God wills to happen happens, and whatever He wills not to happen does not happen. 4) God is the Creator of everything.[4]

Certain sectarian Christians hold similar fatalistic views to those of *Al-Qadar*. Beverly wrote:

To Muslims, Allah is the transcendent eternal Creator who is beyond comprehension. This vision of God leads to an emphasis on predestination and the total sovereignty of God. Islam is more Calvinistic in its outlook than John Calvin! In fact, some Calvinists have pointed to Islamic doctrine as proof that Calvin was correct since "even pagan Muslims see the truth about predestination." [5]

Conceivably, a Muslim man could be cast to Hell, while a Christian is welcomed into Paradise, if it be Allah's will. That would go against everything the Qur'an teaches, and Allah would have contradicted himself, but such contradiction is not out of character or without precedent for Allah. Remember, when Allah gave the Qur'an, he contradicted and abrogated most everything the Bible teaches – teachings he had supposedly revealed.

Judgment Day – The Scales

The picture of this promised Day of Judgment is quite different in Islam versus Christianity. These differences follow closely along the variant lines of the Biblical and Qur'anic teaching on sin and its consequences.

The Qur'an teaches that all men will face the scales. A man's eternal being will be bound, and he will be unable to speak. Then his physical body parts will serve as a witness to Allah, telling all the evils this man committed in life.

"The day the enemies of God will be gathered at the Fire and the records of their deeds will be distributed, So that when they reach it their ears and eyes and persons will testify to what they did. And they will say to their bodies: 'Why did you testify against us?' They will answer: 'God, who gave all things power or articulation, made us speak. It is He who created you the first time, and to Him you will return. You did not hide your (doings) so that your ears or eyes or persons should not testify against you. In fact you thought that God did not know the things you used to do. It is this notion that you had of your Lord that caused your ruin, and you are lost,'" Surah 41:19-23.

"We shall seal their lips that day; and their hands will speak, their feet testify to what they had done," Surah 36:65.

Beyond this hostile, out-of-body experience, books will be produced that have recorded all the deeds of a person's life. The deeds shall be made known, and people will be judged accordingly.

"The ledger (of their deeds) would be placed before them. Then you will see the sinners terrified at its contents, and say: 'Alas, what a written revelation this, which has not left unaccounted the smallest or the greatest thing!' They will find in it whatsoever that had done. Your Lord does not wrong anyone," Surah 18:49.

"We have kept account of everything in a book. So taste (the fruit of what you sowed), for We shall add nothing but torment," Surah 78:29-30.

Once all the testimony is given and the books are read, the deeds are placed in Allah's great scale – good to one side and evil to the other – for the actual judgment to occur. Though the spiritual being is unable to speak, evidently he will see the scale and know his fate. Those whose good deeds are greater than evil deeds will be admitted to Paradise.

"We shall recount (their deeds) to them with knowledge, for We were never absent (and saw all they did). And the weighing will be just on that Day. Then those whose (deeds) are lighter in the scale shall perish for violating Our signs," Surah 7:7-10.

"Only those whose scales are heavier in the balance will find happiness. But those whose scales are lighter will perish and abide in Hell forever. Their faces will be scorched by flames, and they will grin and scowl within it," Surah 23:102-104.

Judgment Day – The Christ

Christians know that on the Judgment Day all people will stand before Jesus Christ whom God has appointed to execute judgment, John 5:27-29; Matthew 25:31-32; Acts 17:31; 2 Corinthians 5:10. It will be unnecessary for mortal bodies or body parts to speak out against their owners. The flesh and mortal world will be gone, 2 Peter 3:10-13. All will have been resurrected with a body formed and fitted sufficient for eternal life, John 5:27-29; 1 Corinthians 15:35-53.

According to the Revelation of John, there may indeed be books opened at the Judgment, records of men's deeds, Revelation 20:11-15. However, Revelation is a highly symbolic book, Revelation 1:1, and such imagery may only represent the omniscient Judge before whom all will stand. "These 'books' seem to record the character and deeds of the individual. This is not to say that God keeps literal books, but that there is a record of our deeds and it is not forgotten."[6] The Bible reveals the just verdict that men's deeds merit: Hell, Romans 3:23; 6:23; Revelation 20:12-13, 15. Yet there is another book mentioned – "the Lamb's Book of Life" – that contains names and not deeds, Revelation 20:12, 15; 21:27. The names in it belong to Christians, members of Christ's body, His church, Philippians 4:3; Hebrews 12:23; Ephesians 5:23; 1:22-23.

Their names are not in the Book of Life because of their deeds. By their deeds alone they would be damned like all other men. Instead, their names are in the Book of Life because they are forgiven by the blood of Jesus Christ. Jesus Christ sacrificed Himself, paying the penalty for sin and satisfying the justice of God, Romans 3:23-26; 5:6-10; Galatians 3:13. Jehovah is truly just and will not wink at sin. It had to be paid for and was by Jesus Christ, 2 Corinthians 5:21; Hebrews 9:28; 1 Peter 2:24; 3:18.

In the final analysis, the only thing that matters is your relationship to Jesus Christ. All are guilty of sin and thus deserving of Hell. But have you been forgiven? Is your name written in the Book of Life?

Qur'anic Deliverance – The Five Pillars of Islam
Faith in the Qur'an means that Allah will not save anyone but Muslims, those that travel the "straight path" of Islam and follow the prophet Muhammad. It is required that one become Muslim and perform the five pillars of Islam to go to Paradise. What are the five pillars of Islam?

1. Faith – reciting the *Shahada*

"Only he who surrenders to God with all his heart and also does good, will find his reward with the Lord, and will have no fear or regret," Surah 2:112.

To become Muslim, one need only believe and repeat the confession, "*Ilaha illa Allah. Muhammad rasul Allah*" ("There is no God except Allah. Muhammad is the Prophet of Allah"). It is not a one-time confession. These words will be repeated many times a day, as it is the key verse in nearly every ritual prayer. Muslim parents will whisper the confession into the ears of their babies. It will be recited at the time of a Muslim's death. It is an all-encompassing statement affirming the Unitarian-Monotheism of Allah, as well as the supremacy of Muhammad and his teaching, the Qur'an.

To be a Muslim, one should also:
- Believe that the Holy Qur'an is the literal word of God, revealed by Him.
- Believe that the Day of Judgment (the Day of Resurrection) is true and will come, as God promised in the Qur'an.
- Accept Islam as his or her religion.
- Not worship anything or anyone except God.[7]

2. Prayer – *Salat*

"Praying at fixed hours is prescribed for the faithful," Surah 4:103.

Ritual prayer is held five times a day – dawn, noon, mid-afternoon, sunset, and nightfall. Muslims must prostrate themselves on the ground facing Mecca in certain postures.[8] They will always repeat the *Shahada* and recite the first Surah of the Qur'an, as well as other private supplications. For the *Salat* to count, the Muslims must be ceremonially cleansed, Surah 4:43. There is a proper way for the Muslim to perform ablutions (wash his face and body) in order to pray.[9] They pray in Arabic, even if the native tongue of a Muslim is different.[10] Arabic is the only acceptable language for praying to Allah.

3. Almsgiving – paying *zakat*

"Fulfill your devotional obligations and pay the zakat. And what you send ahead of good you will find with God, for He sees all that you do," Surah 2:110.

The *zakat* is a compulsory annual contribution of at least 2 ½% of a Muslim's income. It is given to the poor and needy. A Muslim can give more as charity and good deeds for the scales, but they should do it secretly. Failure in this almsgiving will cost one Paradise, as *zakat* is tied to a Muslim's salvation in the following verse:

"Those who believe and do good deeds, and fulfill their devotional obligations and pay the zakat, have their reward with their Lord, and will have neither fear nor regret," Surah 2:277.

4. The Fast – *sawm* (fasting) during *Ramadan*

"O believers, fasting is enjoined on you as it was on those before you, so that you might become righteous," Surah 2:183.

Islam's holy month is Ramadan. This is the month that Gabriel came to Muhammad in the caves outside of Mecca. Muslims are to fast completely from sun-up to sun-down for the entire month. They abstain from food, drink, and sexual relations during daylight, and then when the sun goes down, there is celebration and thanksgiving. There are exceptions for the infirmed, however, if keeping the fast would harm them.

5. The Pilgrimage – the *hajj*

"Perform the pilgrimage and holy visit ('Umra, to Makkah) in the service of God," Surah 2:196.

Once in a Muslim's lifetime, he is to travel to Mecca to worship and perform sacred religious rites around the city and at the Ka'bah.[11] Again, exceptions are made for those too poor or infirmed to make the journey, Surah 2:196. It is easier now in modern times to make this journey, but in some nations, people work and save their entire lives in order to make this pilgrimage, perform the ceremonies, and earn their salvation.

Muslims will have to do many other good deeds beyond keeping the five pillars to tip Allah's scales in their favor. However, no Muslim will see Paradise apart from these works. "The five pillars act as a tapestry that gives Muslims a portrait of their task in life, a journey that they hope ends as it began – as a newborn baby free from all sins."[12]

Biblical Conversion – Obedience to the Gospel

The Bible does not teach that sinners are delivered by remembering to do good works (Isaiah 64:6); rather, they are saved by the grace of God. Salvation is by grace and not meritorious works, Ephesians 2:8-10; Titus 2:11-14. The power of God's salvation is the gospel (literally "good news") and a sinner's response to it – faithful obedience, Mark 16:15-16; Romans 1:16; 16:25-26; Ephesians 1:13-14; 2 Thessalonians 1:8-10.

Christianity provides the Savior for sinful mankind in Jesus Christ, Acts 4:12. Christianity provides the mediator, the intercessor between Holy God and sinful mankind in Jesus Christ, 1 Timothy 2:5; Romans 3:26; 5:8; Mark 10:45. Christianity provides reconciliation, in Jesus Christ because sin severs fellowship between God and man, Isaiah 59:1-2; 2 Corinthians 5:17-21. It was God's plan and will for the ages, conceived in the omniscient mind of God before creation, to accomplish all this through Jesus Christ, Ephesians 1:3-11; 3:8-11; Revelation 13:8. Jesus Christ's sacrifice at the cross made atonement and paid for the forgiveness of sins, 1 John 2:2; Romans 3:23-26. God the Son bore the cost for sin by dying on the cross and freely offers salvation to all mankind, Romans 6.23; Matthew 28:19-20; Acts 2:38-39; 2 Thessalonians 2:14.

How does a sinner respond to God's salvation offer? Since Jesus Christ paid the price for sin, He is the Savior. He can offer pardon on any terms He chooses, and these are stipulated in the New Testament. Sinners respond to the gospel in obedient faith, Hebrews 11:6; John 3:16; 14:21; James 2:17-26. They must convert to Jesus Christ and His gospel for their sins to be blotted out, Acts 3:19. The New Testament process of conversion can be stated simply in five points.

1.   Hear the gospel of Jesus Christ, Mark 15:15-16; Romans 10:11-17; Colossians 1:5-6; James 1:21-22; 1 Peter 1:22-25. One must be taught the gospel – its facts, doctrine, testimony, and truth – in order to believe it, Romans 10:17. Thus the gospel must be preached to the entire world, and the feet of those who carry it to others are called "beautiful," Mark 16:15-16; Romans 10:15. People must hear the truth in order to believe it and convert to Christianity.

2.   Faith in the gospel of Jesus Christ, John 3:16; 8:24; Romans 1:16. Once one has heard the good news, they have a choice to believe it and act on it or not. Just as one has the choice to sin and transgress God's will, so also one has the choice to believe on Jesus and seek God's forgiveness. Biblical faith is more than mere mental assent, as Wilson wrote:

> One of my favorite definitions is found in an old Bible encyclopedia. It says faith is "more than a mere assent to the doctrines of the gospel, which leave the heart unmoved and unaffected... or assent of our sinful condition... or assent of the mind to the method by which God justifies the ungodly... but a hearty concurrence of the will and affections with this plan of salvation, which implies a renunciation of every other refuge, and an actual trust in the Savior... to commit the keeping of our souls into His hands, in humble confidence of His ability and His willingness to save us." (Popular and Critical Bible Encyclopedia, Vol. II, pp. 646-647)
>   The definition cited, as well as the Biblical evidence that supports it, implies that faith involves three constituent parts: 1) conviction of the mind; 2) trust of the heart; and 3) surrender of the will. Faith involves the total engagement of the soul: intellect, emotions, and will.[13]

Contrary to popular teaching, a sinner is not saved at the moment of faith. John 1:12 says that believers have the right to *become* children of God. One is not a saved child of God at the point of faith, but they can become one. Furthermore, a sinner is not saved by faith alone, James 2:24. Faith that justifies is active and obedient to the word of God, Galatians 5:6; Ephesians 2:10; Titus 2:14; James. 2:17-25.

3.   Repentance of sins, turning toward Jesus Christ, Luke 13:3; Acts 2:38; 3:19; 2 Corinthians 7:10. Clearly, Biblical faith acts. The first action prescribed for sinners who believe in the gospel of Jesus Christ is repentance. Repentance is simply a "turning around" or "turning over." Repentance is the sinner changing his mind and attitude toward sin. It also includes the sinner changing behavior; he ceases that which is sinful and is remorseful for having sinned against God.

4.   Confession of Jesus Christ, Romans 10:9-10; Acts 8:35-39. The repentant sinner must confess his faith in Jesus Christ. One is confessing his assent and allegiance to Jesus as well as admitting his need for the Savior. While the Bible knows nothing of a "sinner's prayer" (read it cover to cover

and you'll not find a word about a "sinner's prayer"), it does affirm *"that whoever calls on the name of the Lord shall be saved,"* Acts 2:21. This is not accomplished through a "sinner's prayer," but it is accomplished through confession and baptism, Acts 2:21, 38, 40-41; 22:16; Romans 10:9-13.

5.   Baptism into Jesus Christ, Mark 16:16; Acts 22:16; Romans 6:1-4; Galatians 3:27. For sinners today, there is only one baptism connected with their salvation, just as surely as there is only one Lord and one faith, Ephesians 4:5. Baptism is immersion in water – not pouring or sprinkling, but an actual burial in water, John 3:23; Acts 8:36-38; Romans 6:3-4; Colossians 2:12. The New Testament commands the alien sinner to be baptized.

i.   Baptism is for those who repent of sin and turn their life over to the Lord Jesus Christ, Acts 2:38.

ii.   Baptism is for those who will confess their faith in Jesus Christ, Acts 8:36-38.

iii.   Baptism is for those who believe in Jesus Christ, Mark 16:16; Acts 8:12; 16:30-33.

iv.   Baptism is for the sinner's transgressions to be forgiven, Acts 2:38; 22:16.

v.   And baptism is for salvation in Jesus Christ, Mark 16:16; 1 Peter 3:21.

Thus, the "one baptism" of the New Testament is the immersion in water of the repentant sinner based upon the confession of his faith in Jesus Christ for the remission of his sins. The scriptural evidence given bears this definition out. The Bible does not say that a sinner can pray his way into Jesus Christ, but it says clearly one is "baptized into Christ," Galatians 3:27.

Once a sinner has heard the gospel of Christ, believed it, and obeyed its instructions (repentance, confession, baptism), his state has been changed before God. He is forgiven. He is no longer an alien sinner, but a beloved child of God, Galatians 3:26-27; 1 John 3:1-3. He is now born again, a new creation in Jesus Christ, John 3:3-5; 1 Peter 1:23-25; Galatians 3:26-28; 2 Corinthians 5:17. The child of God in Christ must remain committed and live for Jesus Christ, 2 Corinthians 5:9, 14-15; Revelation 2:10. After his conversion, should a Christian err and sin against the Father, he may repent and confess that sin to God in prayer and be forgiven, 1 John 1:5-2:2. While this world may have much tribulation and persecution in store for the followers of Jesus, on the Day of Judgment, it is the names of faithful Christians that are recorded in the Lamb's Book of Life.

This is far superior to the scales of Islam. The cross of Christ shows that Jehovah God is truly just. No sin shall be winked at; justice will be served, Romans 6:23. Either a man has accepted the Savior (Jesus' death paid for his sins), or he has spurned the Savior (he will pay for his own sins). Either way, the justice of God is satisfied because sin is answered.

Like the Qur'an, the Bible has **not** revealed the "weight" of good deeds or sins. That is no matter to Christians though, because a man does not save himself. There are no scales. He must have a Savior. Forgiveness of sins is granted on the terms of the Savior. When a person obeys the gospel (2 Thessalonians 1:9), he is placing his trust in the Savior. He resigns his fate to the Savior's hands, complying with His terms for forgiveness and allows the Savior to save! The hope of salvation is not in an individual's actions, but in the cross of Jesus Christ.

"But God forbid that I should glory except in the cross of our Lord Jesus Christ, by whom the world has been crucified to me, and I to the world," Galatians 6:14.

Jehovah God is not a respecter of persons, Deuteronomy 10:17; 2 Chronicles 19:7; Job 34:17-19; Acts 10:34; Romans 2:11; 1 Peter 1:17. He does not break His word or play favorites. If He has written that there is a Savior, and prescribed the course for man to follow to have salvation, then that is the truth for everyone. He will not change His mind or make exceptions on Judgment Day. People can trust the Bible, and they must decide for themselves whether or not they will accept the Savior by believing and obeying the gospel, Philippians 2:12; Acts 22:16.

Salvation – Who Is Your Savior?

The Bible says there is a Savior, Jesus Christ. Muslims do not offer their own savior, superior to Jesus in some respect. Instead, Islam denies that Jesus saves. It denies that there is any need for a savior at all. Islam asserts:

• There is no savior, because a Muslim can merit his salvation with good works.

Surely the believers and the Jews, Nazarenes and Sabians, whoever believes in God and the Last Day, and whosoever does right, shall have his reward with his Lord and will neither have fear nor regret," Surah 2:62.

"The day He will gather you together on the Day of Gathering, will be the day of Judgment. He who believed and did the right, will have his evil deeds expunged by God and admitted to gardens with rivers flowing by, and abide there perpetually," Surah 64:9-10.

• There is no savior, because there is no intercessor or advocate for men.
"Warn those who fear, through this (QUR'AN), that they will be gathered before their Lord, and they will have none to protect or intercede for them apart from Him. They may haply take heed for themselves," Surah 6:51.

"Take heed of the day when no man will be useful to man in the least, when no intercession matter nor ransom avail, nor help reach them," Surah 2:48.

- There is no savior, because a Muslim can make up for his sins with good deeds.

"Remember that good deeds nullify the bad," Surah 11:114.

Who is your savior? There's a long list of persons who *do not save* in Islam. Jesus is not the Savior in Islam. He is merely an apostle to the Jews, like so many before him. Muhammad is not the savior. He is a warner and the "Seal of the Prophets," but he does not save any. Allah is not really a savior. He is unpredictable yet absolute. While he gives a list of things for Muslims to do in order to be saved, ultimately he saves who he wishes and damns the rest, Surah 2:284. Allah's word is not final, and he is not bound to respect it. The Muslim's savior (if in any sense he has one) is himself.

The Hope of Suicide

If one believes the Old Testament scriptures, as both Christians and Muslims say they do, then one must acknowledge that God has created and fashioned man with eternity in his heart, Ecclesiastes 3:11. Man inherently needs fellowship with God and assurance about the future. God has fashioned creatures that will search for him, though many today are ignorant about what they are looking for, Acts 17:26-27. This world is full of people who clearly are looking to fill a void in their lives. They look in places as varied as entertainment, drugs, alcohol, illicit relationships, world religions, overtime, play-dates, denominationalism, consumerism, and the list goes on. People fill their calendars (in positive and negative ways), yet their hearts remain empty. Eternity remains in the heart, and it can only be satisfied by God.

As this study shows, Christianity meets that need. "Eternity in the heart" is filled by a genuine relationship with the Eternal Father through the gospel of Jesus Christ. Assurance for the future is found in the forgiveness and promises of Jesus Christ. Only Christianity recognizes the severity of sin and provides a solution which satisfies an equally loving and just God. There is the hope of a Savior in Christianity, Hebrews 6:18-19; 1 Peter 1:3; 1 John 3.1-3.

Islam offers no such confidence. Man must save himself. Man's deeds will be weighed in the balance before him, and the good may or may not outweigh the bad. The Qur'an does not so much as clue the Muslim in on what good deeds and sins weigh. Besides the uncertainty of the scale, Allah reserves the right to arbitrarily save or damn one anyway. However, there is one assurance given in Islam: death in Allah's cause.

"He will not allow the deeds of those who are killed in the cause of God to go to waste. He will show them the way, and better their state, and will admit them into gardens with which he has acquainted them," Surah 47:4-6.

The hope of Islam is found in suicide – at least death for Allah's cause. This death has been viewed in different ways since Muhammad led warriors into battle against the Quarysh between Mecca and Medina.

- Muslims who died marauding trade caravans alongside Muhammad died in Allah's cause.
- Muslims who died in the Crusades died in Allah's cause.
- Muslim children who died walking across minefields for Iranian soldiers in the Iran/Iraq wars died in Allah's cause.
- Muslim boys and girls strapping bombs to themselves and running into cafes or riding buses in Jerusalem died in Allah's cause.
- Muslim hijackers crashing their planes into buildings died in Allah's cause.

The reason for death is Muslim hope! The Qur'an's only assurance of Paradise is death in Allah's cause. For the faithful Muslim, this has to sound better than chancing it on the scales. And who could fathom Allah condemning anyone who gave the ultimate sacrifice to spread Islam? The Qur'an states:

"If you are killed in the cause of God or you die, the forgiveness and mercy of God are better than all that you amass. And if you die or are killed, even so it is to God that you will return," Surah 3:157-158.

"Do not say that those who are killed in the way of God, are dead, for indeed they are alive, even though you are not aware," Surah 2:154.

Evidently, other Arabians and the families of fallen Muslim converts blamed Muhammad for the death of loved ones. The following Surah seems to attempt to both comfort families for their loss as well as encourage others to be more militant and follow the example of those who perished in *jihad* (warfare against infidels that Islam may conquer).

"To those who sit at home and say of their brothers: 'They would never have been killed had they listened to us,' say: 'Drive away death from your midst if what you say is true.' Never think that those who are killed in the way of God are dead, They are alive, getting succor from their Lord, Rejoicing at what God has given them of His grace, and happy for those who are trying to overtake them but have not joined them yet, and who will have no fear or regret. They rejoice at the kindness and mercy of God; and God does not suffer the wages of the faithful to go to waste," Surah 3:168-171.

This lesson asks the tough question, "Who is your Savior?" Christianity offers one and with Him there is forgiveness, reconciliation, hope, and assurance. With Islam, you are on your own. The best that your soul can hope for is a violent end to your life. Night and day difference, isn't it?

The Bible is a sufficient unit revealing God's plan through the ages to redeem sinful mankind through the sacrifice of Jesus Christ. Muhammad's revisions and additions to God's plan (found in the Qur'an) only serve to obscure the truth and discourage mankind from knowing their Savior. Be not deceived: There is a heaven to be gained and a hell to be shunned! Will you obey the gospel and allow the Savior to redeem you by forgiving your sins?

Lesson 10 Questions

1. What beliefs do Islam and Christianity share that would lead to a belief in the final judgment at the end of time?

2. According to the Bible and the Qur'an, why will the end of time be a horrible day for most of humanity?

3. According to the Bible, what is sin and what does it do?

4. What do you like or dislike about the Muslim notion that a person can save himself?

5. What do you like or dislike about the Biblical teaching that a person cannot save himself and needs a savior?

6. Why did Jesus die on the cross of Calvary?

7. Does it sound easier to be a Muslim than a Christian? Why or why not?

8. How does one become a Muslim?

9. List the five pillars of Islam and explain what each one is.

10. How does one convert to Christianity?

11. What assurance does the Christian have of his soul's salvation?

12. What assurance can a Muslim have of his soul's admission to Paradise?

13. Why would Muslims seek death in the cause of Allah?

Endnotes

[1] Moser, K.C. <u>The Way of Salvation</u>. Delight, AR: Gospel Light Publishing Company, 1933. p.17.

[2] Moser, p.17.

[3] Caner, Emir Fethi and Ergun Mehmet Caner. <u>More Than A Prophet: An Insider's Response to Muslim Beliefs About Jesus & Christianity</u>. Grand Rapids, MI: Kregel Publications, 2003. p. 123.

[4] Ibrahim, I.A. <u>A Brief Illustrated Guide To Understanding Islam</u>. Houston, TX: Darussalam, 1997. pp. 48-49.

[5] Beverly, James A. <u>Christ & Islam: Understanding the Faith of Muslims</u>. Joplin, MO: College Press, 2002. p. 21.

[6] McMurray, Carl. <u>From Beneath the Altar: A Commentary on the Revelation, with Questions</u>. Indianapolis, IN: Faith and Facts Press, 1993. p. 145.

[7] Ibrahim, p. 53.

[8] For a step-by-step manual (including pictures) of proper prostrations see Lalljee, Yousuf N. <u>Know Your Islam</u>. Elmhurst, NY: Tahrike Tarsile Qur'an, Inc, 1999. pp. 193-197.

[9] For a step-by-step manual (including pictures) of proper ablutions see Lalljee, pp. 183-188.

[10] For a list of the daily prayers to be recited in Arabic as well as their English translation see Lalljee, pp. 193-206.

[11] For a list of the Muslim rites performed in Mecca, see Caner, Emir Fethi and Ergun Mehmet Caner. <u>Unveiling Islam: An Insider's Look at Muslim Life and Beliefs</u>. Grand Rapids, MI: Kregel Publications, 2002. pp. 128-130.

[12] Caner and Caner. <u>Unveiling Islam</u>. p. 130.

[13] Wilson, Mike. <u>Evangelism Toolbox</u>. <u>mike@focusmagazine.org</u>, 2002. p.26.

Lesson 11

Afterlife: Hell, Heaven, or Paradise?

"Blessed be the God and Father of our Lord Jesus Christ, who according to His abundant mercy has begotten us again to a living hope through the resurrection of Jesus Christ from the dead, to an inheritance incorruptible and undefiled and that does not fade away, reserved in heaven for you, who are kept by the power of God through faith for salvation ready to be revealed in the last time," 1 Peter 1:3-5.

Realizing the Goal

The ultimate goal of the Christian's life is entrance into heaven. Their great hope of this lies within the Savior and judge, Jesus Christ, who admits faithful Christians into heaven.

"Be faithful until death, and I will give you the crown of life," Revelation 2:10.

The New Testament warns Christians against the danger of apostasy, Hebrews 6:4-12; 10:26-39. Believers who chose to be obedient to the gospel may choose later to depart from Christ in affection, devotion, or doctrine, Revelation 2:4-5; 3:15-16; Hebrews 10:24-26; James 4:4-5; 1 Timothy 4:1-6; 2 Peter 2; 2 Timothy 4:3-4, 10; Luke 8:4-15. Such defectors from the truth will by no means see heaven, Revelation 22:14. One's soul is not made eternally secure through baptism alone. Faithful devotion and obedience to the Lord must continue throughout the journey of this life.

"Fight the good fight of faith, lay hold on eternal life, to which you were also called and have confessed the good confession in the presence of many witnesses," 1 Timothy 6:12.

Christians are living with eternity in view, Revelation 21:7. In this respect, entrance to Heaven is seen as a crown, like the prize given to ancient runners for completing their course. Christians are running the race of life, with the prize before them being Heaven (1 Corinthians 9:24-27; Philippians 3:7-14), and it is a race run with assurance, Hebrews 10:19-23.

"I have fought the good fight, I have finished the race, I have kept the faith. Finally, there is laid up for me the crown of righteousness, which the Lord, the righteous Judge, will give to me on that Day, and not to me only but also to all who have loved His appearing," 2 Timothy 4:7-8.

"Blessed is the man who endures temptation; for when he has been proved, he will receive the crown of life which the Lord has promised to those who love Him," James 1:12.

Adding up to Paradise

"God has promised men and women who believe gardens with streams of running water where they will abide forever, and beautiful mansions in the Garden of Eden, and the blessings of God above all. That will be happiness supreme," Surah 9:72.

As Lesson 10 explained, Muslims are working their way to Allah's recompense. Allah's abode for the faithful is called *Paradise* (Muhammad's revision of the Biblical heaven).

"The semblance of Paradise promised the pious and devout (is that of a garden) with streams of water that will not go rank, and rivers of milk whose taste will not undergo a change, and rivers of wine delectable to drinkers, and streams of purified honey, and fruits of every kind in them, and forgiveness of their Lord," Surah 47:15.

A Muslim's task is far beyond trust and devotion to a savior. They attempt to save themselves by continuously doing good works, which hopefully will tip Allah's scales in their favor. Unless they perish in the martyrdom of *jihad*, they have no hope or assurance about the future. Allah's whim may send some people to Hell, though they are model Muslims.

For reasonable people to buy into this system (without being coerced), the pay-off would have to be big, as it seems to be a terrible gamble with their souls. Muhammad's revelations are up to the task though, painting a tantalizing picture of Paradise. Man's basest desires are appealed to in Allah's "recompense" to Muslims: Paradise, Surah 52:17-19; 56:22-24.

This World is Not My Home

In this lesson we will examine Biblical and Qur'anic teaching on Heaven, Hell, and Paradise. Where does the soul go after this life?

The word "Paradise" appears three times in the NKJV New Testament. In the Greek language, the word simply means "garden" or "walled-garden." Figuratively then, "Paradise" is applied to the afterlife. Once it seems to indicate a portion of Sheol (the place of the dead), where there is comfort for the deceased, compare Luke 23:43 and John 20:17; see also Luke 16:19-31. Once it is used clearly describing Heaven, the faithful saint's final abode, Revelation 2:7; 22:1-5, 14. And once "Paradise" is used in a difficult passage that could arguably be interpreted as referring to Sheol or Heaven, 2 Corinthians 12:4. Though this word pertains to the Christian's afterlife, it is hardly relatable to the "Paradise" spoken of in the Qur'an. There is good reason for distinguishing the Christian's Heaven and Muslim's Paradise, and hereafter in this lesson "Paradise" *will only be used in designating Muslim doctrine about the afterlife.*

Christians and Muslims are looking for a very different afterlife. Islam is a religion tied to the material world in many respects: great emphasis is placed upon the body being ritually cleansed; the number of prayers a Muslim must perform, as well as performing them in the correct posture and direction; dietary regulations; sanitary regulations; clothing regulations; good moral character and charitable treatment toward the poor. Islam is largely about the body and less about the soul. Little of the religion is about spiritual fulfillment or one's relationship with God. This is because Allah is transcendent, and such familiarity is blasphemous to Muslims. Allah is a rule-maker. The Qur'an's picture of Paradise is no exception. For a religion that is focused on the body, the Paradise Muhammad spoke of is an appropriate consummation!

Paradise is a place of mortal pleasure. But what do mortal senses matter in a realm of immortality? The Bible's Heaven and Qur'an's Paradise are night and day different. The differences underscore the alternative outlooks of these religions. Christianity is about the spiritual (unseen reality), and Islam is about the carnal (seen reality). Christianity views this life as temporary, a façade and foreshadow of the spiritual universe, experienced in the afterlife, 2 Corinthians 4:16-5:7; 1 Corinthians 15:46-49. Islam sees the afterlife in identical terms as the present life, only intensified: Paradise will be the best physical pleasure one could imagine while Hell will be the worst physical torture one could devise.

Paradise – Every Mortal Need Satisfied

At first, the description of Paradise in the Qur'an echoes the beautiful imagery of the Christians' grand ideal of Heaven. A Christian today can barely imagine the comfort that John's Revelation must have brought first-century Christians suffering prejudice, torture, and deprivation for their Lord. The symbol of Heaven was the New Jerusalem: God's city with glory, grandeur, and beauty captured in the value of precious stones and metals, Revelation 1:1; 21:9-22:5. It was opposite in every way from their wretched temporal state – suffering persecution.

Well, in the Arabian desert of the mid-seventh century, carving out an existence was perilous. Many nomadic Arabians attacked trade caravans as a major source of wealth and sustenance. Water was a precious commodity, and the few oases that the desert offered were prized properties. The sun was unforgiving, while the nights were cold. Very little vegetation was ever seen, only the golden dunes of sand.

Arabians knew both hunger and thirst. They were acutely aware of the painful life where basic physical needs are barely met. The Paradise that Islam offered keyed into this standard of living. Notice how, for the chosen Muslim, Paradise means that every mortal need is met with abundance. Paradise is the garden, the great oasis, far from the desert's heat. Paradise is the easy life with water, shade, vegetation, abundance of food, and servants.

"Announce to those who believe and have done good deeds, glad tidings of gardens under which rivers flow, and where, when they eat the fruits that grow, they will say: 'Indeed they are the same as we were given before,' so like in semblance the food would be. And they shall have fair spouses there, and live there abidingly," Surah 2:25.

"Surely those who fear and follow the straight path will be in a place of peace and security in the midst of gardens and of springs dressed in brocade and shot silk, facing one another. Just like that. We shall pair them with companions with large black eyes. They will call for every kind of fruit with satisfaction," Surah 44:51-55.

"But those who believe and do good deeds We shall admit into gardens with streams of running water, where they will abide forever, with fairest of companions and coolest of shades," Surah 4:57.

"We shall give them fruits and meats, and what they desire," Surah 52:22.

In the Bible, there are clues given within the text to help readers understand whether the Holy Spirit is speaking literally or figuratively. The "streets of gold" in Revelation should be understood as symbolizing the unparalleled wealth and glory of God. This is not an arbitrary statement because Revelation 1:1 says that the entire book was communicated in signs. But it is not easily determined whether Muhammad is speaking literally or figuratively in his "revelations." It is possible that the above verses are symbols of perfection put in terms that people could at least begin to grasp. If that is the case, there is nothing all that objectionable about this view of the afterlife. But Muhammad's "revelations" do not stop here.

Heaven – Mortal Needs Eliminated Altogether

There is a difference in prophesying a future where every carnal need is satiated and one where carnal needs are ceased. The Bible makes it clear that in the spiritual afterlife of Heaven, the weaknesses and desires of the flesh will be removed. There will no longer be toil or want. The needs of the flesh – along with its desires and temptations – will have vanished.

"And I heard a loud voice from heaven saying, 'Behold, the tabernacle of God is with men, and He will dwell with them, and they shall be His people, and God Himself will be with them and be their God. And God will wipe away every tear from their eyes; there shall be no more death, nor sorrow, nor crying; and there shall be no more pain, for the former things have passed away,'" Revelation 21:3-4.

"They shall neither hunger anymore nor thirst anymore; the sun shall not strike them, nor any heat; for the Lamb who is in the midst of the throne will shepherd them and lead them to living fountains of waters. And God will wipe away every tear from their eyes," Revelation 7:16-17.

Heaven is the place of reunion with God and His children, Revelation 21:22-23. The apostle Paul warned about forsaking that spiritual abode for carnal appetites.

"For many walk, of whom I have told you often, and now tell you even weeping, that they are the enemies of the cross of Christ: whose end is destruction, whose god is their belly, and whose glory is in their shame -- who set their mind on earthly things. For our citizenship is in heaven, from which we also eagerly wait for the Savior, the Lord Jesus Christ, who will transform our lowly body that it may be conformed to His glorious body, according to the working by which He is able even to subdue all things to Himself," Philippians 3:18-21.

Yet Muhammad appeals to the carnal appetites of men. His vision of Paradise far exceeds mere ease of life with abundant water, shade, wealth, and food. As the Qur'an goes on, Paradise is a place for Muslim men to indulge in the carnal gratification they denied themselves in this life.

Paradise – The Ideal Turns Sensual

Islam declares fornication to be a sin, though polygamy is allowed, Surah 4:3. The number of wives for Muslim men was limited to four. In their lifetime, Muslim men would limit themselves to four wives or less, making them acceptable before Allah.

But Paradise promises Muslim men the grandest sexual gratification. Allah has created special women, called *houris*, whose sole purpose in existence is pleasuring the Muslim faithful. Surrounded by women and houris, the Muslims have no limitation on the number they may have, and no obligations toward marriage. The Qur'an does not explicitly say that there will be seventy-two virgins given to Muslim martyrs, as you have probably heard in the news. However, that number was not just plucked out of the sky. One of the Hadiths states, "The smallest reward for the people of Paradise is an abode where there are 80,000 servants and 72 wives"[1]

"And with them maidens of modest look and large lustrous eyes, like sheltered eggs in a nest," Surah 37:48-49.

"They would recline on couches set in rows, paired with fair companions (clean of thought and) bright of eye," Surah 52:20.

"And companions with big beautiful eyes like pearls within their shells, As recompense for all they had done," Surah 56:22-24.

In the Koran, he [Muhammad] repeatedly redefines Judeo-Christianity's *heaven* as an enormous God-owned bordello in the sky. In that heavenly brothel, loyal Muslim men – especially those paying the door price of martyrdom – would find a host of virgins, called *houris*, who would forever satisfy all their sexual cravings, see Koran 38:51; 44:54; 55:55-74; 56:22, 34-36. In fact, sex with beautiful houris in heaven was guaranteed to be far more enjoyable than any sex Muslim men might miss by being killed while serving God or by trying to have promiscuous sex here on Earth.[2]

"And maidens incomparable. We have formed them in a distinctive fashion, and made them virginal, loving companions matched in age, for those of the right hand," Surah 56:34-38.

Muslim scholars tend to find a deeper meaning behind these words. One interpretation: heavenly houris are a rare, incomparable and distinctive kind of virgin precisely because, once deflowered, they become physically virginal again for the next sex act.[3]

"How many favours of your Lord will then both of you deny? – In them good and comely maidens […] Houris cloistered in pavilions […] Undeflowered by man or by jinn before them […] Reclining on green cushions and rich carpets excellent," Surah 55:69-76.

Heaven – Carnal Desires Eliminated Altogether

As Jesus taught on sexuality and the afterlife, He said that such relations are only part of this present world, Mark 12:18-27. The sexual component of human bodies will not be a factor in the life to come.

"Jesus answered and said to them, 'Are you not therefore mistaken, because you do not know the Scriptures nor the power of God? For when they rise from the dead, they neither marry nor are given in marriage, but are like angels in heaven,'" Mark 12:24-25.

The Biblical portrait of Heaven is a place eternal, imperishable, and immortal, 1 Peter 1:3-5; Matthew 6:19-20; 1 Corinthians 15:50-57. Nothing about the present world can be described in those terms. Heaven is for spiritual beings. Muhammad's pitch for Paradise amounts to this: Deny your temptations presently, and in the future you may indulge. The Paradise that the Qur'an describes promises the "lust of the flesh," originating from the love of "the world." The Bible declares that the world will pass away, 1 John 2:15-17. Such will not be retained in Heaven. The Bible teaches to deny ungodly lusts for the hope of Christ's appearing.

"For the grace of God that brings salvation has appeared to all men, teaching us that, denying ungodliness and worldly lusts, we should live soberly, righteously, and godly in the present age, looking for the blessed hope and glorious appearing of our great God and Savior Jesus Christ," Titus 2:11-13.

Lasciviousness and fornication are sinful before God, Colossians 3:5-6. God does not change, and neither will His attitude toward these activities. Heaven is not a place where God throws His word out the window and allows His people to behave as prodigals. Heaven promises something far better than lust of the flesh: unbroken fellowship with God, Revelation 21:3-4, 22-23.

How Long Will it Last?

This is not a trick question. The Bible says that the faithful Christian's unbroken fellowship with the Lord will be unending:

"Then we who are alive and remain shall be caught up together with them in the clouds to meet the Lord in the air. And thus we shall always be with the Lord," 1 Thessalonians 4:17.

However, the Paradise of Muhammad is only *possibly* eternal. The one constant with sovereign Allah is his propensity to change. Originally, Muslims were told they would be in Paradise forever, Surah 4:57. But remember, Allah changes his word, changes his rules, and he may well change Paradise or end it completely.

"Those who are blessed will be in Paradise, where they will dwell so long as heaven and earth survive, unless your Lord wills otherwise: This will be a gift uninterrupted," Surah 4:108.

Will Women be Admitted to Paradise?

Western women have complained from time to time, "It's a man's world." If they would read the Qur'an, they would surely complain that "it's a man's after-world." Women are scarcely mentioned in Paradise, except of the *houri* variety. Yet Muslim women do have the potential to tip Allah's scales in their favor.

"God has promised men and women who believe gardens with streams of running water where they will abide forever, and beautiful mansions in the Garden of Eden, and the blessings of God above all. That will be happiness supreme," Surah 9:72.

"Verily men and women who have come to submission, men and women who are believers, men and women who are devout, truthful men and truthful women, men and women with endurance, men and women who are modest, men and women who give alms, men and women who observe fasting, men and women who guard their private parts, and those men and women who remember God a great deal, for them God has forgiveness and a great reward," Surah 33:35.

Muslim women will have to chance their eternal destiny at the scales, though. According to the Hadith, Muslim women are not to be involved in *jihad*. The *hajj* (pilgrimage to Mecca) is their *jihad*, their holy struggle.[4] But this struggle does not offer the same assurance and reward as the martyr's death.

One wonders if the allure of Paradise appeals to Muslim women as strongly as Muslim men. The Qur'an is silent about equitable gratification for women. Regardless of what Paradise holds in store for Muslim women, they would have to prefer it to the alternative of Hell.

Residents of Hell

Christianity and Islam are agreed that ultimately there is no third destination for souls. The Bible teaches Heaven and Hell, while the Qur'an declares Paradise and Hell. It has been demonstrated that Paradise and Heaven are not the same place, but Islam and Christianity both promise the severest punishment for the wicked. Their abode is called Hell. As was observed when comparing Heaven and Paradise, the Bible and Qur'an describe Hell differently. Muhammad picked-up on and perpetuated certain Biblical images of Hell (particularly fire), but took it upon himself to expound and elaborate in the most horrendous terms of torture.

The Infidel's Hell

"But those who disbelieve and deny Our revelations are residents of Hell," Surah 5:86.

Who does the Qur'an say will inhabit Hell? In absolute terms, whoever Allah has determined to be in Hell will be there, Surah 6:18. However, Muhammad's Qur'an is more specific.

Some of Mohammed's hell-threats target only those who disobey God. Read further and the basis for damnation widens. Anyone who rejects his claim to be a prophet or questions the divine inspiration of the Koran is also doomed to eternal flame. Anyone who refuses to go to battle for Islam or retreats from a battle for Islam draws down the same threat, see Koran 8:16 and 9:49.[5]

The infidels and Muhammad's detractors will be in Hell. There are two classes of people who will find themselves in Hell that we would do well to note:

First, those who retreat during jihad will be in Hell. The Muslim's holy war is an all-or-nothing proposition. If they die in the cause of Allah, then their deliverance to Paradise is immediate and sure, Surah 2:217-218. However, if at the crucial moment of the battle (or terrorist attack or suicide bombing) they forgo martyrdom, then they have sealed their fate for Hell.

"For any one who turns his back on that day, except to maneuver or rally to his side, will bring the wrath of God on himself, and have Hell as abode; and what an evil destination!" Surah 8:16.

Eternal fate is a powerful manipulative tool to gain "holy warriors." It insures that once *jihad* has been declared it will only end with victory or death. This spiritual incentive is far more potent than any political ideology. Militant Muslims believe they are fighting for the highest stakes: Paradise or Hell.

Second, those who commit *shirk* – associating anything of the creation with the Creator Allah – will be in Hell. This is particularly poignant for Christians, because Muslims contend Jesus was created, and Christians are guilty of *shirk* for worshipping Him as Lord.

"They are surely infidels who say: 'God is the Christ, son of Mary.' But the Christ had only said: 'O children of Israel, worship God, who is my Lord and your Lord.' Whosoever associates a compeer with God, will have Paradise denied to him by God, and his abode shall be Hell; and the sinners will have none to help them," Surah 5:72.

"The Christians say: 'Christ is the son of God.' That is what they say with their tongues following assertions made by unbelievers before them. May they be damned by God: How perverse are they!" Surah 9:30.

This fundamental teaching about *shirk* is ingrained in Muslim children from the earliest age. As Christians seek to share the gospel of Jesus with Muslim neighbors and co-workers, they must be mindful that much of the message constitutes the rankest blasphemy to Muslim ears. Many Muslims are convinced that the teachings of Christians will lead souls to Hell.

What was Muhammad's vision of Hell? What did he tell Muslims it would be like? Exploring the Qur'an reveals that Muhammad spoke of Hell with the same carnal bent he used to describe Paradise. Hell is pictured in graphic terms of horrific torture: boiling water, suits of pitch, and searing flesh. Muhammad spoke of Hell often in the Qur'an, but the following verses are representative and make the point:

"Before him is Hell, and he will get putrid liquid to drink. He will sip it, yet will not be able to gulp it down. Death will crowd in upon him from every side, but die he will not. A terrible torment trails him," Surah 14:16-17.

"This is Hell, the sinners called a lie. They will go round and around between it and boiling water," Surah 55:43-44.

"You will see the wicked on that day bound together in chains. Of molten pitch shall be their garments, their faces covered with flames," Surah 14:49-50.

"These two (believers and unbelievers) are disputants, who contend about their Lord. But they who disbelieve will be fitted out with garments of flames. Boiling water will be poured down over their heads which will dissolve every thing within their bellies, and their skins. There are iron maces for them. As often as they try to escape from its anguish they would be put back into (the fire), and taste the torment of burning," Surah 22:19-22.

Islamic teaching about Hell emphasizes physical pain. Some Muslims say that the description of Hell is more symbolic, yet others teach that the residents of Hell will have their skin burned-off and then replaced again and again, so they will always feel the pain fresh. Obviously they understand these verses as the literal reality of Hell.

The Sinner's Hell

The Bible teaches that Hell, first and foremost, is the place for the devil and his angels.

"Then He will also say to those on the left hand, 'Depart from Me, you cursed, into the everlasting fire prepared for the devil and his angels," Matthew 25:41.

There is a popular notion that Hell is the kingdom of the devil. The Bible does not teach that he reigns or is in charge of all the eternal punishments. Hell is not the devil's playground; it is his eternal punishment, Matthew 25:46; Revelation 20:10. No being desires to go to Hell. It was prepared to fulfill God's just condemnation upon the devil and other spiritual beings who chose to serve the devil over and against God, 2 Peter 2:4. When human beings sin against God, they align themselves with Satan, becoming his children, Romans 3:23; John 8:44; 1 John 3:8. As such, unpardoned sinners will share the devil's fate before the just and Almighty God, Romans 6:23; Matthew 10:28.

The Bible's revelation of Hell is a place of anguish and torment for immortal beings. While Hell is called the lake of fire (Revelation 20:15), the Bible does not conjure up notions of replacing skin and drinking boiling water. In the resurrection, all beings will have bodies suitable for eternal existence, John 5:26-29. God had the ability to burn a bush without consuming it in this world with all its natural laws, Exodus 3:1-3. Certainly, in the next world the wicked creatures of Hell can experience the wrath of God without any marring of their immortal bodies, Colossians 3:6; Romans 5:9; 1 Thessalonians 1:10. Nothing can make Hell cease. There is no corruption or death of the immortal body that would allow relief for even a moment, Matthew 25:46; Mark 9:43-48.

The Bible teaches that Hell is the final and eternal home of the wicked. Divine justice is meted out through the damnation of Hell.

- Hell is prepared for the devil, his angels, and his followers – sinners, Matthew 25:41; Revelation 20:10; 21:8; 22:15.
- Hell is the Lord's just wrath and vengeance upon the wicked, Isaiah 34:8-10; 2 Thessalonians 1:6-9; Colossians 3:6; Romans 5:9; 1 Thessalonians 1:10.
- Hell is the outer darkness of weeping and gnashing teeth, Matthew 8:10-12. There is no light because God is not there; He is the light of Heaven, Revelation 22:5. There is weeping and gnashing of teeth because there is no hope or comfort; God is comforting the children of Heaven, Matthew 5:4; Revelation 7:17; 21:4.
- Hell is the worm that does not die, Mark 9:43-48.
- Hell is the lake of fire, Revelation 20:10, 15. There will be unquenchable flame, fire, and brimstone, Revelation 14:10-11; 21:8; Mark 9:43-48.

The case for Hell is not overstated with scenes of brutal torture or demonic beings gleefully inflicting pain upon infidels. The simple truth of God's justice served on immortal beings is sobering enough. What grace to be offered forgiveness and escape from such perdition. What terror to forsake such an offer. If the promised glory of heaven is not enough to inspire one to seek the Lord, surely the alternative of Hell will bring one to call out for the Savior.

How Long Will Hell Last?

The New Testament teaches that Hell is an eternal abode, Mark 9:43-48; 2 Thessalonians 1:8-9. It will last as long as heaven does for the saints – forever, Matthew 25:46. Jesus is trustworthy, His word is true.

Again, the Muslim may find comfort in the notion that Hell may not last forever. Some or all of its residents may be released or vanish from existence. Or they may stay there indefinitely. There is a contradiction in the Qur'an about this. Which scripture will Allah choose to respect?

"But those who deny and reject Our signs will belong to Hell, and there abide unchanged," Surah 2:39.

OR

"And those who are doomed, will be in Hell: For them will be sighing and sobbing, Where they will dwell so long as heaven and earth endure, unless your Lord will otherwise. Verily your Lord does as He wills," Surah 11:106-107.

Who Chooses Heaven or Hell?

The God of the Bible does not desire anyone to be lost in Hell, 2 Peter 3:9. While He cannot deny His justice, neither can He deny His love. Both must be satisfied as He deals with humanity. Both **were** satisfied at the cross of Jesus Christ, Romans 3:23-26. Jesus shed His blood for the remission of sins, Matthew 20:28; 26:28; John 1:29. This sacrifice satisfied God's justice, and Christ's gospel satisfies God's love, 1 John 2:1-2; Romans 1:16; John 3:16. What greater expression of love could God make? John 3:16; 1 John 4:8-10.

The gospel of Jesus Christ gives humanity the choice, Acts 2:39; Revelation 22:17; Acts 22:16; Matthew 7:13-14. They may choose to accept the savior, obey the Gospel, and await the unbroken, unending divine fellowship of Heaven: Or they may choose to disregard the gospel and neglect this great salvation, 2 Thessalonians 1:8-9; Hebrews 10:26-31.

The choice is yours, and God will eternally respect your decision.

Allah, on the other hand, chooses who enters Paradise and who goes to Hell. He has given the scales which might sway his decision, but he will choose regardless. The choice is removed from humanity, as the following verses show:

"God leads whosoever He wills astray, and shows whoever He wills the way: He is all-mighty and all-wise," Surah 14:4.

"God invites you to mansions of peace, and guides whosoever He will to the path that is straight," Surah 10:25.

This study has always mentioned that these religions are exclusive. One cannot adhere to the one without absolute rejection of the other. But for a moment, consider the implications of having a choice in your eternal destiny.

If the Bible is the truth, you cannot be saved without being a Christian. You must choose to obey the gospel and be saved. However, if Islam is true, you are delivered to Paradise by Allah, whether you are a Muslim or not. Allah is absolute and arbitrary. You have nothing to lose in forsaking Islam, but everything to gain in embracing the gospel of Jesus Christ!

Lesson 11 Questions

1. Does the Bible teach that a child of God cannot sin so as to lose his salvation? Explain your answer.

2. What hope does a Christian have about the future?

3. What expectations would Muslims have about their future? What assurances are given in the Qur'an?

4. What are features of Islam's Paradise?

5. Do you think it's fair to say that the Muslim's concept of Paradise is sensual? Why or why not?

6. In what ways does Heaven differ from Paradise?

7. Who chooses the soul's destination in these religions?

8. To you, which version of Hell sounds worse? Why?

9. Specifically, who does the Qur'an condemn to Hell?

10. Arguably, the existence of Biblical Hell can serve as an immediate motivation for people to choose the Savior. What immediate purposes does the existence Islam's Hell serve?

Endnotes

[1] Caner, Emir Fethi and Ergun Mehmet. More Than A Prophet: An Insider's Response To Muslim Beliefs About Jesus & Christianity. Grand Rapids, MI: Kregel Publications, 2003. p. 152.

[2] Richardson, Don. Secrets of the Koran. Ventura, CA: Regal Books, 2003. p. 38.

[3] Richardson, p. 38.

[4] Caner, Ergun Mehmet and Emir Fethi Caner. Unveiling Islam: An Insider's Look At Muslim Life And Beliefs. Grand Rapids, MI: Kregel Publications, 2002. p. 194.

[5] Richardson, p. 93.

Lesson 12
Spreading the Word:
A Matter of Life and Death?

"And take the helmet of salvation, and the sword of the Spirit, which is the word of God," Ephesians 6:17.

Two Domains – The Kingdom or the World
The inspired apostle Paul spoke of two realms into which humanity is divided: the domain of darkness and the kingdom of the Son.

"He has delivered us from the power of darkness and translated us into the kingdom of the Son of His love, in whom we have redemption through His blood, the forgiveness of sins," Colossians 1:13-14.

One must live as part of Christ's kingdom – a member of His blood-bought body, the church which He saves, Matthew 16:18-19; Acts 20:28; Ephesians 1:22-23; 5:23. Otherwise, one lives under the sway of the lusts of this world and the prince of the air, the devil, Ephesians 2:2-3; John 14:30; 16:11; 1 John 2:15-17. This concept can be stated in several ways:

- You are a citizen of the kingdom, or you are part of the dominion of darkness, Colossians 1:13-14; Philippians 3:18-21.
- You are a member of the church, or you are a party to the world, Ephesians 2:12-13; Colossians 2:20; 1 Corinthians 1:2; Acts 2:40-41, 47.
- You are living in Christ, or you are dead in trespass and sin, Ephesians 2:4-5; Galatians 3:27.
- You are a child of God, or you are a child of the devil, 1 John 3:1-2, 8, 10.

It is important to remember that God has no grandchildren. No one inherits the relationship and reconciliation that Christians have with God through Jesus Christ. Each person must believe and obey the gospel for themselves, exercising their choice to accept the gracious salvation found in Jesus. Christians are not better than their counterparts in the world, but they are better off, because they have been forgiven and added to the church, Acts 2:38, 47.

The word "church" in the English Bible comes from the Greek word EKLESSIA, meaning "a called-out assembly." The Lord's church consists of those called by the gospel out of the world and into God's fellowship, 2 Thessalonians 2:14. The primary work of His church is for the members to sound out the gospel call to the world, allowing others the opportunity to come to God and end their allegiance to the world, Matthew 28:18-20; Mark 16:15-16; John 17:11-21. The borders of Christ's kingdom expand one soul at a time.

> "[…] *I write so that you may know how you ought to conduct yourself in the house of God, which is the church of the living God, the pillar and ground of the truth,*" 1 Timothy 3:15.

As Christians work to spread Christ's kingdom, they do this through evangelism, the preaching of the gospel. It is the word of truth, the gospel, which saves people, Romans 1:16; Colossians 1:5-6. Christianity is about saving souls. When the gospel is taught, it inspires genuine love, and motivates obedience to Christ. The New Testament does not command nor exemplify physical militancy, coercion, terror, or torture to advance Jesus' cause. Jesus seeks genuine conversion and there is nothing genuine about forcing another's will.

The kingdom of Christ is not of this world. Therefore, Christianity can be preached and its doctrines followed under any government arrangement. Christians can live and stand acceptable before God under democracies, dictatorships, monarchies, Communist states, or Islamic theocracies. New Testament teaching never called for overtaking a government-regime, but commanded saints to live peaceably with all men and obey all the laws of the land, so long as they do not cause one to sin against God, Romans 12:17-18; 13:1-7; 1 Timothy 2:1-5; Acts 5:27-32. In times past, certain nations decided they did not want Christians in their borders and persecuted the saints. But believers are told to follow the example of Jesus, suffer the persecution, and continue to preach and practice righteousness, 1 Peter 2:19-24; 3:13-17; 4:12-19; Revelation 2:8-11.

Two Abodes – Islam or War

Likewise, Islamic doctrine teaches that there are two domains or abodes among the followers of Allah:

> Islam divides the peoples of the world into two distinct realms or abodes: the Abode of Islam and the Abode of War. The former have submitted to the will of Allah, and the latter are still resisting. Countries under Muslim control are considered the Abode of Islam. It is the duty of all Muslims to preserve the Abode of Islam from contamination and, where possible, to enlarge it at the expense of the Abode of War, where the "infidel" rules.[1]

At the time of this writing, at least thirty-two nations around the globe could say they were in the abode of Islam, or *ummah* (the community of all those who affirm Islam), with an eighty percent or greater Muslim population.[2]

While the Abode of Islam is promoted through teaching, there are other tactics embraced by Muslims spreading the word of Allah. There are three evident strategies in diminishing the Abode of War, as well as safeguarding and spreading the Abode of Islam, captured in the following three Arabic words:

- *Da'wah* – Islamic evangelism and "mission" work
- *Jihad* – Holy War against infidels
- *Shariah* – Muslim code of law created by combining Qur'anic and Hadith commands as applied to the state.

Da'wah

Strictly speaking, *Da'wah* means "invitation" or "calling." However, as Jane I. Smith, professor of Islamic Studies at Hartford Seminary wrote, *Da'wah* is a much nuanced Arabic word. She lists three different definitions for the word:

1. *Da'wah* means the active business of the propagation of Islam with the end of making conversions.
2. *Da'wah* involves the effort to bring those who have fallen away from Islam back to active involvement in the faith.
3. *Da'wah* means the responsibility to simply live quiet lives of Muslim piety and charity, with the hope that by example they can encourage wayward coreligionists as well as others that Islam is the right and appropriate path to God.[3]

The Qur'an instructs Muslims to be witnesses to the world of the message of Muhammad, Surah 2:143. Christians can respect the three versions of *Da'wah* listed above, as they mirror the Biblical standard and strategy of evangelism. Christians are to be honest in their dealings with others, and should work at instructing non-Christians in the faith, John 14:6; Ephesians 4:25; Colossians 3:9-10. However, the Qur'an and Hadith teach a double-standard about honesty toward infidels. Muslims are not strictly enjoined to be honest in their dealings with non-Muslims. This has applications in everything from business deals to converting "coreligionists" to Islam. Wagner writes:

> When a Muslim tries to win someone to the Islamic faith, the use of truth is not always the best way to proceed. If a praiseworthy aim is attainable through the telling of a lie, then this is allowed. There is no more praiseworthy aim than that of bringing someone to an acceptance of Islam.
>
> Many who have carried out business transactions with Muslims have been surprised to see that the deal has been built on deceit. The grounds given for such is that lying is permitted when on a journey, and the journeys during the time of Muhammad were almost always business trips. Therefore, in business, the truth may not always be accepted when the common good is to be achieved. The question comes not in ethics of lying, but in what is the common good. The person telling the lie generally defines the common good.[4]

Such situational honesty allows Muslims the freedom to spread Islam in overt and public forums, as well as in covert and near-secretive ways. Wagner refers to *Da'wah* as "The Quiet Revolution,"[5] and surveys successful avenues of *Da'wah* in free Western nations such as the United States.[6]

• **Target the Academic World with Islam.** In recent years, great efforts have been made to expose Western youth to Islamic doctrine in both elementary and secondary education systems under the heading of "Multicultural Studies" (or in the case of universities, departments of "Islamic Studies"). Wealthy Islamic nations (such as Saudi Arabia) have endowed financially troubled institutions to erect "Islamic Study Centers" or buildings to house an "Institute of Religion." Muslim professors are trained and sent to teach in universities around the world, spreading Islam on campuses. The American disposition toward pluralism allows Islam to be promoted in Western schools while Christianity is barred. For some reason, freedom of speech, intellectual freedom, and freedom of religion are extended to Islam in the public education system, but not to Christianity. "Islam has taken advantage of American openness and has made great progress in *Da'wah* in our schools that are closed to Christianity. The educational institutions of the West will be a major battleground for Islam in the future."[7]

• **Target Prisons with Islam.** "It is estimated that more than 300,000 prisoners are converts to Islam, and that the rate of conversion may be more than 30,000 each year."[8] There are now Muslim chaplains who minister to Islamic communities in correctional facilities. Some of the appeal of Islam to inmates is thought to be the immediate changes affected by conversion: taking a new Muslim name, adhering to Muslim hygiene and diet, and acceptance into the prison's influential Islamic population.

• **Target Minorities with Islam.** "Islam is focusing on people groups in America and the West and is creating strategies to meet the needs of these target peoples. As of now the numbers are not large, but as Christians have learned, people who feel displaced or alienated are more open to conversion than those who have deep roots. The minorities in America fit into this category."[9] Muslims are focusing on blacks, Latinos (whose population now exceeds blacks in the U.S.) and Native Americans, stressing Islam's teaching of charity and social equitability.

• **Target Urban Centers with Islam.** Muslims are in building programs. An average of one new mosque opens each week in the United States.[10] By erecting large and beautiful mosques in cities, they raise the profile of Islam and communicate its strength, affluence, and acceptability as a religious option. Mosques are centers for Islamic life. The congregations of local Muslims meet there for prayer, instruction, and strategy in further *Da'wah*.

Jihad

When Americans try to capture the essence of Muslim propagation in a single word, likely they think of the term *jihad*. In the West, Muslims are likely to win far more converts through *Da'wah*, but it is *jihad* that makes the headlines, enrages nations, and incites both fear and curiosity for Islam. What does *jihad* mean? What does the Qur'an teach? Do all Muslims practice *jihad*? Do they practice it alike?

Jihad can be defined simply as "Holy War." However, most Muslims use *jihad* in the sense of a "personal struggle." Consider what the following sources had to say:

> *Jihad* has two connotations: greater and lesser. The greater is the function of the individual who must strive constantly to live up to the requirements of the faith. The lesser is primarily a community function and thus, an obligation. The idea of *jihad* in a military context with its emphasis on the notion of continuous struggle against non-believers in God tended to keep alive the spirit of solidarity in the community over and against outsiders. While the Qur'an does not make of *jihad* in the "holy war" context an article of faith, it is the *Hadith* which renders it into a formula for "active struggle" that invariably tended toward a militant expression. The incentive for *jihad* lies in its two-fold benefits: booty for this life and martyrdom with its immediate promise for a blissful eternal hereafter for those killed in battle, the *shuhada* (sing. *shahid*: martyr).[11]

> The average Muslim follows jihad only in the sense of personal struggle. Frankly, most are as terrified by the sectarian violence as are non-Muslims. Those living in the West are personally caught in the backlash by those angered by the work of extremists. Those living in Islamic societies are anxious because Muslim radicals from another sect or extreme fringe may choose to attack their countries. [...] The extremists hold that those who refuse to pick up guns and bombs are indeed cowardly and without genuine fidelity to Islam.[12]

> In both the Qur'an and the Hadith, the infidel (kafir) must be converted or conquered. Muslims who die in the struggle against infidels (jihad) will immediately be translated to the highest level of Paradise. Much of this doctrine draws on admonitions and injunctions in the Hadith, but strong Qur'anic foundations exist for holy war.[13]

As with "Christendom" and the Bible, so also various sects of Muslims read the Qur'an differently. Most Muslims read passages about "war," "struggle," "fight" only in the sense of personal battles with temptation and transgression. They suggest that perhaps such carnal warfare was necessary and practiced by Muhammad in the harsh Arabian frontier, but now it is only metaphor for the struggle of personal purity. Islam today is really about peace, and has evolved from such brutality. Other Muslims read the same verses as clear precepts and mandates which can be obeyed or disobeyed as easily as *Salat* or confessing the *Shahadah*. These fundamental readers are often labeled "extremists" or "militant," and are responsible for terrorism perpetrated in the name of Allah the world over.

Peace, Peace

Such Muslim groups as the Kharijites and the Ibadis believe in jihad so intensely that they consider it the sixth pillar of Islam. Others, however, have publicly and privately repudiated jihad as warfare. In particular, Sufi sects such as the Qadiriya and the Indian Chishtiya have banished the doctrine of warfare from their Islamic theology. The problem is that many Sunni and Shi'ite Muslims do not accept the Sufi as true Muslims. Sufi themselves are vulnerable targets of violent persecution. For that matter, any prominent Muslim who openly speaks of peace is in constant danger of being killed. Extremists perceive that such a blasphemer has been compromised by exposure to the West.[14]

As with so many other issues raised in this study, the Qur'an furnishes "revelations" that support both sides. One wonders which verses Allah intended to abrogate:

"There is no compulsion in matter of faith. Distinct is the way of guidance now from error. He who turns away from the forces of evil and believes in God, will surely hold fast to a handle that is strong and unbreakable, for God hears all and knows every thing," Surah 2:256.

What other application of Surah 2:256 could be made than that Islam is a religion of peace and tolerance? Muslims must be especially sensitive to other viewpoints and beliefs, lest they overstate their case and inadvertently compel someone of a "co-religious" viewpoint to convert to Islam, right? However, the apparent teaching of Surah 2:256 is not even consistent throughout Surah 2! Read on:

"Fight those in the way of God (who fight you), but do not be aggressive: God does not like aggressors. And fight those who fight you wheresoever you find them, and expel them from the place they had turned you out from. Oppression is worse than killing. Do not fight them by the Holy Mosque unless they fight you there. If they do, then slay them: such is the requital for unbelievers," Surah 2:190-191.

"Fight them till sedition comes to end, and the law of God (prevails). If they desist, then cease to be hostile, except against those who oppress [...] So if you are oppressed, oppress those who oppress you to the same degree, and fear God, and know that God is with those who are pious and follow the right path," Surah 2:193-194.

Allah tells Muslims, through Muhammad, that something distasteful can often build one up. Unfortunately, for peace-loving Muslims, it was war that was decreed for them, whether they liked it or not.

"Enjoined on you is fighting, and this you abhor. You may dislike a thing yet it may be good for you; or a thing may haply please you but may be bad for you. Only God has knowledge and you do not know," Surah 2:216.

"O Prophet, urge the faithful to fight. If there are twenty among you with determination they will vanquish two hundred; and if there are a hundred then they will vanquish a thousand unbelievers, for they are people devoid of understanding," Surah 8:65.

As a Christian and a citizen of the United States of America, this writer is personally grateful that most Muslims are peaceful and choose to interpret the violent verses in the Qur'an metaphorically. However, from a textual standpoint (just reading the Qur'an), the basis for this decision is unseen. What clues lie within the book to suggest that any of Muhammad's precepts concerning *jihad* are optional or symbolic? What special revelation do these peaceful Muslims have that allows them to discern which commands are abrogated and which are not?

Militant Muslims contend that the "peaceful verses" have been abrogated by the "war verses," and they make a strong case. Richardson catalogued 109 war verses in his extensive study of the Qur'an that are left unchallenged, unanswered, and un-abrogated.[15] Richardson writes, "Verses that mention war in storytelling (e.g. "David slew Goliath" in 2:251) are not included. Nor are verses in which "God" afflicts infidels – *if Muslims did not help him!*"[16] 109 verses of the Qur'an direct Muslims to physical violence against infidels in Allah's cause.

Ayatollah Khomeini led Iran into the Abode of Islam by indoctrinating and encouraging the country's Muslim population to oust the Shah (the secular government) through religious revolution. Khomeini left no doubt that an Islamic religious revolution will ultimately bear arms. The Qur'an does not teach that evil is overcome by good – rather, evil is overcome by militancy! Khomeini said:

> Those who know nothing of Islam pretend that Islam counsels against war. Those who say this are witless. Islam says, "Kill all the Unbelievers" just as they would kill you. Islam says, "Kill them, put them to the sword and scatter their armies." Islam says, "Kill in the service of Allah." Whatever good there exists is thanks to the sword, and the shadow of the sword. People cannot be made obedient except by the sword. The sword is the key of Paradise, which can only be opened for Holy Warriors.[17]

Whether all Muslims choose to read and follow the violent prescriptions of the Qur'an or not, it cannot be denied that the book teaches these things. Furthermore, in a religion where Paradise is earned solely on the basis of works, it seems illogical to conclude that direct commands (injunctions) are poetic or symbolic language. It is not surprising that some Muslims act out violently in accord with the directions of their holy book. It is simple obedience. This presents a definitive difference between Christians and Muslims on how they are told to treat their enemies and the enemies of God.

A Different Treatment of Enemies

> • **Personal Enemies.** The Qur'an encourages Muslims to seek personal retaliation and vengeance for wrongs inflicted upon them or Allah's cause.

"Permission is granted those (to take up arms) who fight because they were oppressed. God is certainly able to give help to those who were driven away from their homes for no other reason than they said: 'Our Lord is God.' […] God will surely help those who help Him, - Verily God is all-powerful and all-mighty," Surah 22:39-40.

Christians were given the exact opposite instruction. They are to love their enemies, help and pray for their enemies, and remember that "vengeance is the Lord's," Luke 6:27-28; Romans 12:19-21. This difference should remind all people of the difference between Jehovah God and Allah. Jehovah loves His enemies (though He will judge them justly), while Allah hates His enemies (and will judge them arbitrarily along with faithful Muslims).

> • **Spiritual Enemies.** The Qur'an encourages Muslims to destroy any people who actively oppose their faith.

"You tell the unbelievers in case they desist whatever has happened will be forgiven them. If they persist, they should remember the fate of those who have gone before them. So, fight them till all opposition ends, and obedience is wholly God's. If they desist then verily God sees all they do," Surah 8:38-39.

"So when you clash with the unbelievers, smite their necks until you overpower them, then hold them in bondage. Then either free them graciously or after taking a ransom, until war shall have come to end. If God had pleased He could have punished them Himself, but He wills to test some of you through some others. He will not allow the deeds of those who are killed in the cause of God to go to waste," Surah 47:4.

Christians are taught to suffer and endure persecution brought against them by those who actively oppose their faith, Matthew 5:10-12; 1 Peter 3:14-16.

> • **National Enemies.** The Qur'an also constitutes civil law for Islamic theocratic states (*Shariah* law). Its pages provide authority for waging warfare against the enemies of an Islamic republic.

"But when these months, prohibited (for fighting), are over, slay the idolaters wheresoever you find them, and take them captive or besiege them, and lie in wait for them at every likely place. But if they repent and fulfill their devotional obligations and pay the zakat, then let them go their way, for God is forgiving and kind," Surah 9:5.

"Fight those people of the book who do not believe in God and the Last Day, who do not prohibit what God and His Apostle have forbidden, nor accept divine law, until all of them pay protective tax in submission," Surah 9:29.

Ali includes this note about the "protective tax" mentioned in Surah 9:29: "*Jaziyah* is a tax levied on non-Muslims for protection and other services."[18] Protection from whom? This tax was paid by non-Muslims so that they could have some protection from the law and not be arrested or persecuted for their beliefs.

The Bible teaches Christians that the word of Jesus is the law of His spiritual kingdom, His church, John 18:36, Matthew 26:51-53. As such, there is no provision made authorizing punishment or warfare against national enemies. The church is a spiritual body, not a nation-state.

Why Do Some Muslims Fight?

Western media have poked fun at the Muslim understanding of Paradise (heaven) – virgins for men to enjoy and so forth – but it is much more significant to recognize that dying in jihad is the only way a Muslim can be assured of entering Paradise at all. This is why you see Muslims leaving their own nations to fight jihad in other countries. Their motivation is religious, which is much more dangerous than a political motivation.[19]

The Qur'an's only assurance of Paradise is the martyr's death in *jihad*. And it curses the fearful and faithless Muslim to Hell who shows cowardice in the face of *jihad*.

"They ask you of war in the holy month. Tell them: 'To fight in that month is a great sin. But a greater sin in the eyes of God is to hinder people from the way of God, and not to believe in Him, and to bar access to the Holy Mosque and turn people out of its precincts; and oppression is worse than killing. They will always seek war against you till they turn you away from your faith, if they can. But those of you who turn back on their faith and die disbelieving will have wasted their deeds in this world and the next. They are inmates of Hell, and shall there abide for ever. Surely those who believe, and those who leave their homes and fight in the way of God, may hope for His benevolence, for God is forgiving and kind,'" Surah 2:217-218.

Is Allah's Cause Advanced by *Jihad*?

The Qur'an teaches that Islam should be promoted by the sword, and it is evident that Muhammad believed in and practiced this conquer-to-convert tactic.

In essence, Muhammad said, "Convert or die." He declared, "I have been ordered [by Allah] to fight the people till they say: None has the right to be worshipped but Allah, and whoever said it then he will save his life and property," Hadith 2:483. [...] Muhammad's mission was to conquer the world for Allah. The goal of jihad, or a holy war, is to establish Islamic authority over the world. Islam teaches that Allah is the only authority, and all political systems must be based on Allah's teaching. Allah is important.[20]

This teaching and practice is condemned by both New Testament instruction and Western sensibilities. Nevertheless, *jihad* is a method of spreading Islam that the Qur'an enjoins on Muslims.

A Beam in the Christian's Eye?

Jesus taught that before one can correct another with a small fault in their life, he must be sure that he is not guilty of the same or even greater error, Matthew 7:3-5. This does not condemn intervention, but rather hypocrisy, 1 Corinthians 10:12; Galatians 6:1-2; James 5:19-20. Some Muslims would not accept that Christianity is so peaceful and long-suffering in its nature. They point to examples in history – such as the Inquisition and Crusades – to conclude that violence is found in every religion.

> Much of the Muslim and Western media broadside against Christianity links it with the Inquisition and the Crusades as if these were still in progress. That is an illogical but handy device to lure public attention away from the fact that radical Islam's jihad is *current, active, and ongoing.* This is a "now" thing. Again and again we hear the statement, "One can find violence in all religions." Far more pertinent is the closely closeted question: Which religion, if any, is perpetrating violence *now?*
>
> This leads to other equally pertinent questions: *Which religion, if any, tends to be violent because its founding scriptures authorize violence? Which religion, if any, has to violate its own founding scriptures in order to resort to violence?*[21]

Other Muslims might look on the Bible as a whole and say that Jehovah God was a God of war in the Old Testament. Consider Joshua's campaign in Canaan, for example. Isn't this *jihad*? The answer is no. Joshua and other Old Testament Israelite leaders never battled pagan nations in order to proselytize them. Which Old Testament scripture indicates that Joshua's campaign was waged because the Canaanites were not Israelis? Or shows that Joshua would have staid his hand had Canaanites converted to the Law of Moses? When did Joshua send messengers into a besieged city offering peace on the terms of wholesale conversion?

The conquest of Canaan recorded in Joshua was violent. However, it was not an evangelistic strategy. The sovereign Jehovah God used the nation Israel as His instrument to visit judgment on other nations. As one continues studying the Old Testament, it is seen that God does the same thing to the nation Israel later on, using Assyria and Babylon to conquer the Israelites and carry them out of Canaan as captives. Joshua is not a book of *jihad*. There is no conquer-to-convert strategy at work.

Joshua is an Old Law issue anyway. Jesus Christ was the ultimate sacrifice, fulfilling and finishing the Law of Moses, effectively nailing it to His cross, Matthew 5:17-18; Luke 24:44-47; John 1:29; 19:28-30; Colossians 2:13-17. Old Testament practice does not dictate nor authorize Christian faith and practice. Christians are amenable to the New Covenant, the gospel of Jesus Christ, Matthew 28:18; Colossians 3:17. Richardson got it right when he wrote:

> In the future, I hope Christian spokespersons will be clearheaded enough to answer [...] "Sir, I am not an Israelite of Joshua's time. I am a Christian who lives by the New Testament. Quote me a New Testament war verse if you can, and I will reply."[22]

Shariah Law

When Muhammad escaped Mecca for Medina, he soon rose to prominence as an arbitrator and adjudicator between the tribes of the area. His "prophethood" entitled him to be a legal figure as well as a spiritual leader, and some of the revelations Allah sent him at Medina pertain to handling various tribal disputes. By the end of Muhammad's life, he was the leader (spiritual, militarily, and judicial) of the Arabian Peninsula. His revelations combined with his edicts constituted the original *Shariah* law of Arabia. "The death of Muhammad may be considered to have ended constitutional legislation in orthodox Islam."[23]

> The *Shariah* encompasses legislation derived from the Qur'an and the *Hadith*. Tradition and the juridical consolidation of life molded under the stimuli of the Qur'an and the *Hadith*, with no distinction between spiritual and temporal law, served to rally the believers throughout the Muslim world. [...] The *Shariah* is Islam's constitution.[24]

Once a nation becomes a Muslim republic – that is, Islam is declared the national religion – *Shariah* law is to follow. This is faithful restoration to Muhammad's pattern. The abode of Islam was a state centered in Mecca during the Prophet's lifetime but in subsequent centuries, wars and western-colonialism decentralized it. However, wherever Muslims constitute a majority of citizens in a country, their faith will call for *Shariah* law to rule. Modern examples of Islamic republics adhering to *Shariah* law have been Iran under Ayatollah Khomeini, Afghanistan under the *Taliban*, Saudi Arabia, and Sudan.

Once a nation is governed by *Shariah* law, then the state is preserving and promoting Islam. In many respects the face of that nation reverts to seventh century Arabia.

- In clothing – Example: Women must wear veils, or in some cases body-coverings called *burkhas*.
- In worship – Example: Loud speakers throughout towns will call for *Salat,* and all will make prayers toward Mecca together.
- In justice – Example: A hand will be severed as just punishment for theft. Preferred methods of capital punishment include beheading and stoning. Shariah law also means that the nation will follow the Qur'an's edicts concerning

treatment of non-Muslims living within their borders. This does not bode well for "infidels" such as Christians and Jews. According to the Qur'an, it is permissible for the Islamic state to banish all the infidels from its borders. The following verse serves to "legalize" brutal treatment of non-Muslims:

"The punishment for those who wage war against God and His Prophet, and perpetrate disorders in the land, is to kill or hang them, or have a hand on one side and a foot on the other cut off, or banish them from the land. Such is their disgrace in the world, and in the Hereafter their doom shall be dreadful," Surah 5:33.

As the Qur'an often reminds the reader, Allah is merciful and kind. One such "mercy" is seen in that death is not automatically pronounced upon the infidel. Actually, an Islamic republic can be partially hospitable to Christians and the like in their lands, so long as the infidels can pay for protection. The *Jaziyah* tax is levied on non-Muslims.

"Fight those people of the book who do not believe in God and the Last Day, who do not prohibit what God and His Apostle have forbidden, nor accept divine law, until all of them pay protective tax in submission," Surah 9:29.

As long as the tax can be paid, non-Muslims need not fear official state-sponsored persecution. However, non-Muslims are not full citizens, and little will be done to safeguard them or their property from militant Muslims living around them.

Shariah law creates nations with their wealth, armies, resources, lands, and seats in the world community that are wholly dedicated to increasing the Abode of Islam while diminishing the Abode of War by whatever means are necessary and deemed prudent.

It Shall Stand

The kingdom of Christ will stand forever. Even death cannot conquer it, Matthew 16:18-19. The Christian's God is a consuming fire.

"Therefore, since we are receiving a kingdom which cannot be shaken, let us have grace, by which we may serve God acceptably with reverence and godly fear. For our God is a consuming fire," Hebrews 12:28-29.

But the kingdom of Jesus is spiritual; it is not of this world, John 18:36. Christians are citizens and subjects of the most High, King of kings and Lord of lords, Jesus Christ. Service to Jesus demands honesty in the Christian life, and especially in evangelistic efforts, because only the truth can set one free, John 8:31-32; 14:6. Jesus abhors violence done in His name, Matthew 26:51-54; John 18:36. There is nothing in the New Testament which even hints that Jesus commanded or exemplified violent measures to force others to follow Him. Also, Jesus never envisioned a national

Christian state. He had the opportunity to become a national leader (John 6:15), as well as a world leader (Luke 4:5-8), and He passed. Instead, He chose the shame of the cross and has been exalted to the throne on high, Hebrews 1:1-4; Ephesians 1:20-23; Colossians 1:16-18; Philippians 2:5-11.

Christians gladly spread the gospel of a risen Savior and reigning King Jesus! Christians are called soldiers in the New Testament, but they do not war against fleshly armies – they war against spiritual principalities, Ephesians 6:10-17; 1 Timothy 2:3-4; 2 Corinthians 10:3-5. Christians do take up a sword, but it is the sword of the Spirit, God's holy word, Ephesians 6:17; Hebrews 4:12. Christians must always contend for the faith and the true gospel, but never by resorting to violence or bloodshed, Jude 3; Galatians 1:6-8; Hebrews 12:14.

Both Islam and Christianity agree that spreading the word is a matter of life and death. The Qur'an encourages a violent death in this life for all who reject the word of submission. Christianity suffers long and warns of the second death, which is God's judgment of Hell awaiting those who, by their own free will, reject the gospel of Jesus Christ, Revelation 20:6, 14; 21:8.

Lesson 12 Questions

1. What are the two domains of Christianity?

2. What are the two abodes of Islam?

3. How do the "domains" and "abodes" compare?

4. What do Christians do to try and bring other people out of the world and into Jesus' kingdom?

5. What strategies does the Qur'an promote to diminish the "Abode of War?"

6. What does *Da'wah* mean?

7. List particular areas of Western society that *Da'wah* efforts target.

8. Do you think Muslims will be more successful converting people through *Da'wah* or *jihad*?

9. What do most Muslims understand to be the application of Qur'anic passages that command warfare?

10. How do Jehovah and Allah differ when it comes to their enemies?

11. How should Christians treat personal enemies? Give scriptures.

12. How should Christians treat people of different faiths? Give scriptures.

13. What is *Shariah* law?

14. How do countries change when they enact *Shariah* law?

15. Give some examples of modern Islamic republics that abide by *Shariah* law?

16. What kinds of things does *Shariah* law allow Islamic states to do to non-Muslims living within their borders?

Endnotes

[1] Goldmann, David. <u>Islam and the Bible</u>. Chicago, IL: Moody Publishers, 2004. p. 20.

[2] Wagner, William. <u>How Islam Plans to Change the World</u>. Grand Rapids, MI: Kregel Publications, 2004. pp.247-262.

[3] Smith, Jane I. <u>Islam in America</u>. New York, NY: Columbia University Press, 1999. p. 160.

[4] Wagner, p. 126.

[5] Wagner, pp. 39-59.

[6] The following bullet points summarize material presented in Wagner, pp. 46-57.

[7] Wagner, p. 49.

[8] Wagner, p. 50.

[9] Wagner, p. 57.

[10] Rhodes, Ron. <u>Reasoning from the Scriptures with Muslims</u>. Eugene, OR: Harvest House, 2002. p. 7.

[11] Farah, Caesar E. <u>Islam</u>. 6th Ed. Hauppauge, NY: Barron's, 2000. p. 154.

[12] Caner, Emir Fethi and Ergun Mehmet Caner. <u>More Than A Prophet: An Insider's Response to Muslim Beliefs About Jesus & Christianity</u>. Grand Rapids, MI: Kregel Publications, 2003. pp. 250-251.

[13] Caner, Emir Fethi and Ergun Mehmet Caner. <u>Unveiling Islam: An Insider's Look At Muslim Life And Beliefs</u>. Grand Rapids, MI: Kregel Publications, 2002. p. 185.

[14] Caner and Caner, <u>More Than A Prophet</u>. p. 251.

[15] Richardson, Don. <u>Secrets of the Koran</u>. Ventura, CA: Regal Books, 2003. p. 254.

[16] Richardson, p. 253.

[17] Wagner, p. 23.

[18] Ali, Ahmed. <u>AL-QUR'AN: A Contemporary Translation</u>. Princeton, NJ: Princeton University Press, 2001. p. 165.

[19] Gabriel, Mark A. <u>Islam And Terrorism</u>. Lake Mary, FL: Charisma House, 2002. p. 29.

[20] Goldmann, David. <u>Islam and the Bible</u>. Chicago, IL: Moody Publishers, 2004. p. 22.

[21] Richardson, p. 136.

[22] Richardson, p. 137.

[23] Farah, p. 157.

[24] Farah, pp. 155-156.

Lesson 13
Night and Day (Review)

"You are all sons of light and sons of the day. We are not of the night nor of darkness," 1 Thessalonians 5:5.

Night and Day

Ali's rendering of Surah 3:140 is uniquely poetic when compared to other English translations of the Qur'an. While all the translations communicate the same message, Ali brings out the contrast of the affairs of men in the hands of Allah with the phrase "night and day."

"If you have been wounded they too have suffered a wound. We cause this alternation of night and day in the affairs of men so that God may know those who believe, taking some as witness (of truth) from your ranks, for God does not like those who are unjust," Surah 3:140.

As this study began, four goals were set: 1) Receive a clear presentation of Islam and Christianity from primary sources (the Bible and the Qur'an) for both these works are understandable by their own admission (Surah 12:1-3; Ephesians 3:1-5; 5:17); 2) Gain an appreciation of the first principles of both faiths (their history, claims, and precepts); 3) Identify definitive differences; and 4) Discover the implications of committed discipleship to these mutually exclusive religions.

By opening the Bible and the Qur'an and letting them speak for themselves, it was demonstrated that Islam and Christianity are fundamentally different and exclusive faith-systems. They are not sister faiths; promoting such a notion is, at best, misinformation.

The student is encouraged to review the material in Lessons 2, 3, and 4 from time to time when preparing to discuss Islam or Christianity with others. It is important to be aware that many in current Western society reject the notion of absolute truth and favor pluralism. Qur'anic Islam and Biblical Christianity contend there is truth. The early lessons in this study serve as a foundation, as there should be familiarity with the standards of authority that Christians and Muslims will appeal to in order to justify their faith and practice. Are the Bible and the Qur'an both trustworthy and reliable, or are there differences? Can they be read and applied by the same standard, or are there differences? Do they stem from the same origin, or are there differences? It is hoped that these lessons can be springboards for the student's future study and exploration of these religions.

Returning to Surah 3:140, this verse provides a platform for a succinct five-point comparison and review of Christianity and Islam. The following five areas speak deeply to the personal implications of committed faith to either Islam or Christianity:

"If you have been wounded..." – Militancy or Peace?[1]

These words of comfort (?) are directed to Muslims who have paid a physical price in advancing the cause of Allah. It would be frustrating and demoralizing for *jihadin* (Holy Warriors)[2] to suffer a loss in battle and not die. Death in Allah's cause is the only assurance of Paradise, Surah 2:154; 3:157-158.

But why do Allah's devout men fight at all? Why wage carnal warfare against Christians, Jews, idolaters – any people of variant faith-systems? Allah through the Qur'an enjoined this militant behavior.

"Enjoined on you is fighting, and this you abhor. You may dislike a thing yet it may be good for you; or a thing may haply please you but may be bad for you. Only God has knowledge and you do not know," Surah 2:216.

"O Prophet, urge the faithful to fight. If there are twenty among you with determination they will vanquish two hundred; and if there are a hundred then they will vanquish a thousand unbelievers, for they are people devoid of understanding," Surah 8:65.

"Fight those in the way of God (who fight you), but do not be aggressive: God does not like aggressors. And fight those who fight you wheresoever you find them, and expel them from the place they had turned you out from. Oppression is worse than killing. Do not fight them by the Holy Mosque unless they fight you there. If they do, then slay them: such is the requital for unbelievers," Surah 2:190-191.

"Fight them till sedition comes to end, and the law of God (prevails). If they desist, then cease to be hostile, except against those who oppress [...] So if you are oppressed, oppress those who oppress you to the same degree, and fear God, and know that God is with those who are pious and follow the right path," Surah 2:193-194.

Thankfully, most Muslims (and especially those living in the West) refuse to literally abide by Muhammad's precepts. However, reasonable people can read them and understand their significance. It is disturbing to note that the four quotations given can be multiplied twenty-five times over and more in the pages of the Qur'an.[3]

Physical peace and longsuffering is enjoined upon the followers of Jesus Christ in the pages of the New Testament, Matthew 5:10-12; 1 Peter 3:14-16. Christians may be physically wounded while suffering various persecutions at the hands of the enemies of God, but not because they instigated conquer-to-convert tactics in the hope of a heavenly reward, Acts 5:40-42. Christians may lose their life (suffer martyrdom) in order to find it, but they will not take life to secure their place in heaven, Matthew 10:38-39; 26:52.

"They too have suffered a wound…" – Retaliate or Suffer Persecution?[4]

Islam cannot abide the idea of Allah or his people suffering a loss in the eyes of this world. The *jihadin* are encouraged: that if they are wounded, how much more the infidel! Personal retaliation is acceptable and promoted in the Qur'an.

"Permission is granted those (to take up arms) who fight because they were oppressed. God is certainly able to give help to those who were driven away from their homes for no other reason than they said: 'Our Lord is God.' […] God will surely help those who help Him, - Verily God is all-powerful and all-mighty," Surah 22:39-40.

Christians are given the exact opposite instruction. They are to love their enemies, help and pray for their enemies, and remember that "vengeance is the Lord's," Luke 6:27-28; Romans 12:19-21. This should help remind all of the difference between Jehovah God and Allah: Jehovah loves His enemies (though He will judge them justly), while Allah hates His enemies (and will judge them arbitrarily along with faithful Muslims).

Jesus suffered physical shame and wounding for the sake of others, Isaiah 53:5; 1 Peter 2:21-24; Hebrews 12:2; Galatians 3:13. The twelve apostles themselves, as well as many Christians of the first century, suffered terrible, painful persecution and loss. Their comfort was never to be found in retaliation and the glory of this world, but in the arms of their Father in the heavenly abode, Hebrews 11:30-40; Revelation 6:9-11; 12:11.

"We cause this alternation […] in the affairs of men…" – Determinism or Choice?[5]

The Islamic doctrine of Allah's sovereignty is such that Allah determines and predetermines everything. Whether a Muslim experiences good fortune or bad, his response ever should be "Allah wills it," because Allah caused it. This is evident in Allah's judgment upon souls. While Muslims are working hard to merit their salvation on Allah's scales by good works, ultimately Allah chooses who resides in Paradise and Hell regardless of a human's disposition toward him.

"To God belongs all that is in the heavens and the earth; and whether you reveal what is in your heart or conceal it, you will have to account for it to God who will pardon whom He please and punish whom He will, for God has the power over all things," Surah 2:284.

"To God belongs all that is in the heavens and the earth: He may pardon whom He please and punish whom He will. Yet God is forgiving and kind," Surah 3:129.

Allah causes everything, both good and evil, Surah 113:1-2. Jehovah God, on the other hand, created beings with freewill. While He is certainly sovereign, He has endowed human beings with the dignity of choice, and He loves them enough to respect their choices. Some choose to do evil in the sight of the Lord, while others choose to receive salvation in Jesus Christ by faithful obedience to His gospel.

Sin is your choice, Romans 3:23; Isaiah 59:1-2. Accepting forgiveness in Jesus Christ and living faithfully for Him is also your choice, Acts 2:40; 22:16; Matthew 7:13-14; Philippians 2:12. How will you choose?

"So that God may know those who believe..." – Saved by Works or by Grace?[6]
Muslims have the difficult task of attempting to save themselves from Hell. They must merit their Paradise by doing more good deeds than bad in the course of their lifetime. This begins with (but would not be limited to) keeping the five pillars of Islam. At Allah's judgment, all their deeds, both good and evil, will be put on the scales.

"Remember that good deeds nullify the bad," Surah 11:114.

"We shall recount (their deeds) to them with knowledge, for We were never absent (and saw all they did). And the weighing will be just on that Day. Then those whose (deeds) are lighter in the scale shall perish for violating Our signs," Surah 7:7-10.

"Only those whose scales are heavier in the balance will find happiness. But those whose scales are lighter will perish and abide in Hell forever. Their faces will be scorched by flames, and they will grin and scowl within it," Surah 23:102-104.

Allah will know who truly believes by the scales. As the previous section pointed out though, will it matter? Will he care? Will he save the Muslim who measures equal? Will he save the one whose scale is just a hair light?

The New Testament does not base salvation on a meritorious works system, Ephesians 2:8-10; Titus 3:4-7. There is a Savior, Jesus Christ (Acts 4:12; John 14:6), and His substitutionary death on the cross offers forgiveness of sins and reconciliation to God, 1 John 2:1-2; John 1:29; Hebrews 9:22; Matthew 26:28; 2 Corinthians 5:18-21. The important thing is having remission of sins in Christ. The Bible clearly teaches sinful men what they must do to be added to the body of Christ and be saved, Romans 1:16; Mark 16:15-16; Acts 2:38-47; 22:16; Galatians 3:26-27; 2 Corinthians 5:17.

"God does not like those who are unjust" – Does God Love?[7]
The Bible says that Jehovah God is love, 1 John 4:8. He does not wait for love to be shown to Him and then reciprocates – God initiates love, 1 John 4:10, 19. One of the greatest truths of the Bible is that God loved humanity despite their grievous sins

against Him. When humanity was helpless and unlovable in every respect, God's love shown forth and acted on humanity's behalf, Romans 5:6-8. Jehovah demonstrated His unconditional love for the world in sacrificing Jesus Christ, John 3:16. The love of Jehovah is not like the love of men. It is perfect, pure, and the standard that Christians strive for, 1 Corinthians 13. Jehovah loves even His enemies, and He always has, Matthew 5:43-48.

Remember, the Qur'an lists many people whom Allah does not love, Surahs 2:190; 2:276; 3:57; 4:36. Jehovah God, nonetheless, loves sinners and seeks to redeem them in Christ, Romans 5:8. Jehovah God loves first (1 John 4:19), while Allah only "loves" those who first love him! Allah does not love his enemies, Surah 2:98. Allah does not initiate love or a loving relationship with sinners. He reciprocates love only for the Muslim who obeys Muhammad. But for the disbeliever (sinner, infidel, Christian), Allah has only hate.

"Say: 'Obey God and His Messenger;' and if they refuse (then remember) God does not love disbelievers," Surah 3:32.

Darkness Settles

"Night and Day" accurately captures the disparity between Islam and Christianity. As greater portions of the world's population (as well as the West) fall sway to the fables and man-made "recitations" of the Qur'an, darkness shall cover their hearts, 2 Timothy 4:2-4. What could a religion that follows an un-loving god (Allah), an un-trustworthy book (Qur'an), and an un-holy prophet (Muhammad) offer the world other than darkness?

All Muslims are told that the true Qur'an can only be understood in Arabic. However, as the religion grows, fewer and fewer of its converts can understand this language. Shrouding the "straight path" in a foreign language perpetuates the darkness. Muslims of other native languages must content themselves with what their Mullahs tell them. This can stymie critical investigation.

Muslims are warned in the Qur'an not to question Islam. They are told that if they do, the answers may not satisfy, and will cause them to lose their faith. Apparently, this is what happened to previous "people of the book," according to the Qur'an. They questioned Allah's will and lost their faith when they received the answers.

"O believers, do not ask about things which, if made known to you, may vex you. But if you ask about them when the Qur'an is being revealed they will be unfolded to you. [...] Such things were asked by a people before you, but they disbelieved afterwards," Surah 5:101-102.

Any teaching that dare not be questioned is suspect! This discourages critical thinking, investigation, and meditation on the Qur'an. Such disciplines would only lead to questions. A book that, when questioned, discourages the faith of followers instead of strengthening it, should not be trusted. This attitude safeguards the darkness of Islam.

Finally, Muslims are told not to befriend Christians or Jews, because such associations will destroy their faith, Surah 3:98-101. Why? What is Allah afraid that the Muslims will hear? This isolation would never serve the truth. If Islam is the truth, Muslims need to befriend erring Christians and Jews to share their doctrine. Instead, Muslims are told only to befriend other Muslims. The following verses feed a sick paranoia that suggests all Jews and Christians have banded together against Muslims.

"O believers, do not hold Jews and Christians as your allies. They are allies of one another; and anyone who makes them his friends is surely one of them; and God does not guide the unjust," Surah 5:51.

"O believers, do not make friends with those who mock and make a sport of your faith, who were given the Book before you, and with unbelievers; and fear God if you truly believe," Surah 5:57.

"Your only friends are God and His Messenger, and those who believe and are steadfast in devotion, and pay the zakat and bow in homage (before God)," Surah 5:55.

Sons of Light

Against the backdrop of Islam, New Testament Christianity shines brightly! Jehovah God put no restrictions on the language used to communicate His word. Instead, the Holy Spirit's example was to allow men to hear it in their native tongue, Acts 2:1-11. God's truth is the truth no matter the language! Jesus Christ never discouraged questions. He told people to "Ask," "Seek," and, "Knock," Matthew 7:7-8. He desired people to grope for the knowledge of God and meditate upon it, Acts 17:27; 1 Timothy 4:15-16. Christians increase their faith by asking questions of God's word; they do not destroy it, Romans 10:17. Because God's word is the truth, Christians are to share it with everyone they meet, Matthew 28:18-20; Acts 8:4. Christians need not fear losing their faith because of exposure to another religion. The Bible (because it is true) guards them against error, darkness, and sin, Ephesians 5:11; 2 Timothy 3:16-17; 2 Peter 1:3.

Christians must be bold to be the light of the world, 2 Timothy 1:7; Matthew 5:14-16; Philippians 2:15-16. Their confession that Jesus is the Christ, the Son of the living God, must be heard from continent to continent, Matthew 16:16. The message of love, hope, forgiveness, and a savior is good news indeed to people whose religion offers none!

Christians must carry the light today – as their ancestors of faith did in the first century – by preaching the word everywhere they go (Acts 8:4); embodying the message in their behavior (Ephesians 5:8-17); and suffering persecution for the faith, 1 Peter 4:16. The saints will have opportunities to speak to Muslims of the gospel in schools, prisons, offices, and neighborhoods. May they be the sons of light they were called to be.

Lesson 13 Questions

1. What do you think are the greatest similarities between Islam and Christianity?

2. List some differences between Islam and Christianity.

3. Do Muslims and Christians pray to the same God? Explain your answer.

4. What are points of common ground between Muslims and Christians that could be used to begin an evangelistic discourse?

5. What questions about Islam or Christianity has this study raised in your own mind that you would like to pursue answers to on your own or in another class? List them.

6. How is salvation fundamentally different in Islam and Christianity?

7. How is "God" fundamentally different in Islam and Christianity?

8. Why do Christians need greater boldness in teaching Muslims the gospel?

9. How did Christians in the first century become effective "lights" to the world?

10. How does hypocrisy hinder the Christian's efforts to teach Muslims and others the gospel?

Endnotes

[1] Review Lesson 12.

[2] Caner, Emir Fethi and Ergun Mehmet Caner. More Than A Prophet: An Insider's Response To Muslim Beliefs About Jesus & Christianity. Grand Rapids, MI: Kregel Publications, 2003. p. 205.

[3] Richardson, Don. Secrets of the Koran. Ventura, CA: Regal Books, 2003. p. 254.

[4] Review Lesson 12.

[5] Review Lesson 10.

[6] Review Lesson 10 and Lesson 8.

[7] Review Lesson 9.

What Good Is A Tract That Nobody Reads?

Check out Spritbuilding's list of eye-catching, visitor oriented tri-fold and four-fold tracts. Biblical in their presentation, they are perfect for tract racks or outreach. People WILL pick these tracts up.

For just a small charge they can be imprinted with
- church name
- and address
- times of services
- logo or message
- or all of the above!

A Scriptural Consideration of Baptism
Are Babies Born in Sin?
Are You Happy?
Do You Feel Alone?
Girls, Why Say No?
Instrumental Music in Worship
Is Tongue Speaking for Today?
Is Your Family Struggling?
Is Your Life Too Complex?
Lost Among the Churches?
Old Law or New, Which?
"Oneness" Pentecostalism
Please Lord Just Add One More Hour…
Realized Eschatology (70 A.D. Theory)
Saved Like A Thief
The Lord's Supper, A Second Serving?
What About Abortion?
What Are You Looking For in a Church?
What Can You Expect When You Vist?
What Is The Church of Christ?
Who Do You Trust?
Why Believe The Bible?
Witchcraft, Just an O.T. Problem?

Order at
www.Spritbuilding.com

All tract titles available also
in spanish.

Spiritbuilding.com …
Spiritual "equipping"
for the contest of life.

Spiritbuilding
Bible Challenge on
CD

- Helps bring the familiarity of computing to Bible class

- Covers the Old and New Testaments in 8 CDs

  ➤ CD #1- The Book of Genesis
  ➤ CD #2- The Exodus, Wandering, Conquest of Canaan
  ➤ CD #3- Judges, Ruth, United Kingdom, Wisdom Literature
  ➤ CD #4- Divided Kingdom, Captivity, Prophets
  ➤ CD #5- Jesus' Early Life and Miracles
  ➤ CD #6- Jesus' Parables, Later Works and Teachings
  ➤ CD #7- Jesus Gives His Life and the Early Church
  ➤ CD #8- Paul's Journey's and the Epistles

- For use in Bible classes, lesson reviews, suppplemental class work, Bible labs, homeschooling, and gaming

- Almost 5,000 Bible questions in a multiple choice format with your choice of easy, medium, or hard questions

- Includes scripture hints and score keeping... students can retake questions to improve score

- Download a free demo at www.EducateGames.com

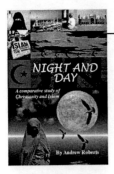

NIGHT AND DAY is a thorough and Biblical comparison between the religion of Islam and New Testament Christianity. This "fastest growing religion in the world" deserves to be examined and understood and Andrew Roberts brings dedication and research to bear on the subject. This study is an update of Andrew's lecture series on this subject. Included are important lessons on authority and the validity of the Bible as the only true Scripture and Jehovah as the only true God. 13 chapters, 150 pages,

A class book for ladies. Cassondra Leigh Givans is a professional newspaper journalist as well as mother and teacher. She has a heart of compassion and outreach that leads her to work with girls in juvenile homes. Now she uses her writing ability to bring that same outward focus to **THE GOSPEL OF JOHN** in a way that women in small group settings will appreciate. 12 chapters with 66 pages.

THE PATH OF PEACE uses the mind picture of a hiker traveling life's path. 12 chapters focus on the choices and decisions facing today's traveler on that path. There are many life shaping decisions that need to be made with seriousness, and the understanding of God's ability to see ahead and warn us.

With sensitivity and scripture the author brings her experience in the juvenile detention facilities to bear on such important topics for young adults as materialism, sexuality, friends, enemies, substance abuse, and anger, as well as topics like one's tongue, justice, compassion, and diligence. 54 pages.

In **EXERCISING AUTHORITY** Author John Baughn has determined to avoid the common presentation of God's authority as it has been narrowly focused on past issues. He has instead focused on the daily and common application of God's authority in the Christian's life.

John's work in the school system and political arena, as well as his reputation as a talented Bible teacher, make him especially qualified to present this vital subject with a little different focus. 12 chapters, spiral bound, 50 pages. Recommended teachers manual to assist in presenting this material,100 pages with suggested answers, group activities, talking points, etc.

Two Bible class workbooks that address real needs for growing Christians.

both are available at www.Spiritbuilding.com

1 & 2 Timothy & Titus

A study guide that is both a workbook for class study as well as a commentary on these personal epistles of Paul. Matthew Allen has done an excellent job with **1&2 TIMOTHY AND TITUS** providing a goodly amount of background material while simultaneously focusing on the relevant aspects of these letters for today. Emphasis throughout is on the personal relationship between Paul and Timothy. The workbook includes references to modern English versions to give additional insight and focus to the study. 13 chapters with 109 pages.

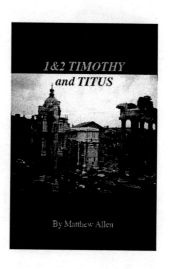

INSIDE OUT

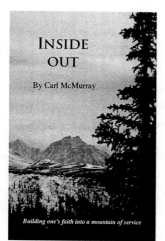

INSIDE OUT is a work book for those who definitely see the need for maturing and growing up in the Spirit led path, but want that path broken down into bite size pieces. Carl McMurray uses scripture, humor, and anecdotal wisdom to motivate growth and the direction of one's personal compass. The author believes firmly that to be a servant of the Most High is indeed one's highest calling and achievement. If we learn how to become faithful servants, we cannot help but to mature into the image of His glorious Son. 12 chapters with 128 pages,

Try any of these other Bible study work-books in the LIVING LETTER SERIES by Frank Jamerson.

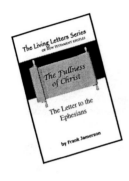

The Gospel of Mark
The Gospel of John
Acts
The Letter to the Romans
1 Corinthians
2 Corinthians
The Letter to the Galatians
The Letter to the Ephesians
Philippians and Colossians
1 & 2 Timothy
1 & 2 Thessalonians
The Letter to the Hebrews
The Letter of James
1 Peter
2 Peter and Jude

Other Bible Study Workbooks by Frank Jamerson

The Godhead
A Study of the New Testament Church
Bible Authority, How Established How Applied

www.Spiritbuilding.com